THE ELEUSINIAN MYSTERIES & RITES

THE ELEUSINIAN MYSTERIES & RITES

BY

DUDLEY WRIGHT

INTRODUCTION BY THE

REV. J. FORT NEWTON, D.LITT., D.D.

Past Grend Chaplain of the Grand Lodge of Iowa, U.S.A.

ISBN: 978-93-5128-769-8(HB)

First Published in 1919
Indian Reprint in 2017

Published by

Kalpaz Publications
C-30, Satyawati Nagar,
Delhi – 110052
E-mail: kalpaz@hotmail.com
Website: kalpazpublications.com
Ph.: +91-9212142040

Cataloging in Publication Data—DK
Courtesy: D.K. Agencies (P) Ltd. <docinfo@dkagencies.com>

Wright, Dudley, 1868-1949, **author.**
The Eleusinian mysteries & rites / by Dudley Wright ; introduction by the Rev. J. Fort Newton.
pages cm
"First published in 1919"—Title page verso.
ISBN 9789351287698

1. Eleusinian mysteries. I. Title. II. Title: Eleusinian mysteries and rites.

BL795.E5W75 2017 DDC 292.9 23

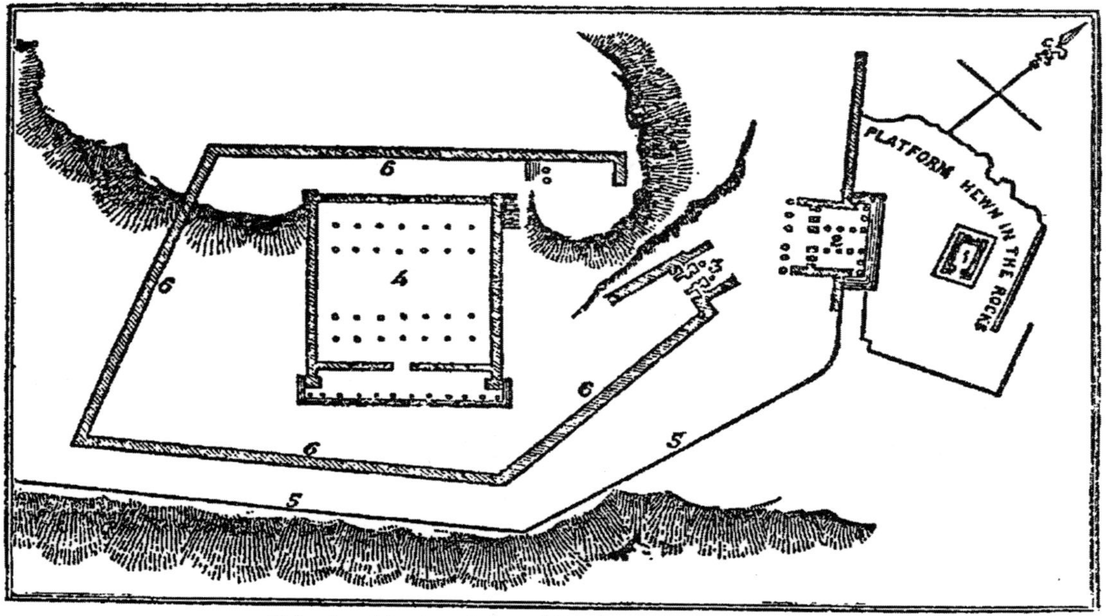

Reproduced by permission of the Encyclopædia Britannica.

PLAN OF THE SACRED BUILDINGS OF ELEUSIS.

1. Temple of Artemis Propylæa.
2. Outer Propylæon.
3. Inner Propylæon.
4. Temple of Demeter.
5. Outer Enclosure of the Sacred Buildings.
6. Inner Enclosure.

PREFACE

AT one time the Mysteries of the various nations were the only vehicle of religion throughout the world, and it is not impossible that the very name of religion might have become obsolete but for the support of the periodical celebrations which preserved all the forms and ceremonials, rites and practices of sacred worship.

With regard to the connection, supposed or real, between Freemasonry and the Mysteries, it is a remarkable coincidence that there is scarcely a single ceremony in the former that has not its corresponding rite in one or other of the Ancient Mysteries. The question as to which is the original is an important one to the student. The Masonic antiquarian maintains that Freemasonry is not a scion snatched with a violent hand from the Mysteries—whether Pythagorean, Hermetic, Samothracian, Eleusinian, Drusian, Druidical, or the like—but is the original institution, from which all the Mysteries were derived.

In the opinion of the renowned Dr. George Oliver: "There is ample testimony to establish the fact that the Mysteries of all nations were originally the same, and diversified only by the accidental circumstances of local situation and political economy." The original foundation of the Mysteries has, however, never been established. Herodotus ascribed the institution of the Eleusinian Mysteries to Egyptian influences, while Pococke declares them to have been of Tartar origin, and to have combined Brahminical and Buddhistic ideas. Others are equally of opinion that their origin must be sought for in Persia, while at least one writer—and who, in these days, will declare the theory to be fanciful?—ventures the opinion that it is not improbable that they were practised among the Atlanteans.

The Eleusinian Mysteries—those rites of ancient Greece, and later of Rome, of which there is historical evidence dating back to the seventh century before the Christian era—bear a very striking resemblance in many points to the rituals of both Operative and Speculative Freemasonry. As to their origin, beyond the legendary account put forth, there is no trace. In the opinion of some writers of repute an Egyptian source is attributed to them, but of this there is no positive evidence. There is a legend that St. John the Evangelist—a character honoured and revered by Freemasons—was an initiate of these Mysteries. Certainly, more than one of the early Fathers of the Christian Church boasted of his initiation into these Rites. The fact that this is the first time that an attempt has been made to give a detailed exposition of the ceremonial and its meaning in the English language will, it is hoped, render the articles of interest and utility to students of Masonic lore.

As to the influence of the Mysteries upon Christianity, it will be seen that in more than one instance the Christian ritual bears a very close resemblance to the solemn rites of the Latin and Greek Mysteries.

The Bibliography at the end does not claim to be exhaustive, but it will be found to contain the principal sources of our knowledge of the Eleusinian Mysteries.

DUDLEY WRIGHT.

OXFORD.

CONTENTS

INTRODUCTION

BY

THE REV. J. FORT NEWTON, D.LITT., D.D.,
Past Grand Chaplain of the Grand Lodge of Iowa.

FEW aspects of the history of the human spirit are more fascinating than the story of the Mysteries of antiquity, one chapter of which is told in the following pages with accuracy, insight, and charm. Like all human institutions, they had their foundation in a real need, to which they ministered by dramatizing the faiths and hopes and longings of humanity, and evoking that eternal mysticism which is at once the joy and solace of man as he marches or creeps or crowds through the welter of doubts, dangers, disease, and death, which we call our life.

Once the sway of the Mysteries was well-nigh universal, but towards the end of their power they fell into the mire and became corrupt, as all things human are apt to do, the Church itself being no exception. Yet at their best and highest they were not only lofty and noble, but elevating and refining, and that they served a high purpose is equally clear, else they had not won the eulogiums of the most enlightened men of antiquity. From Pythagoras to Plutarch the teachers of old bear witness to the service of the Mysteries, and Cicero testified that what a man learned in the house of the Hidden Place made him want to live nobly, and gave him happy thoughts for the hour of death.

The Mysteries, said Plato, were established by men of great genius, who, in the early ages, strove to teach purity, to ameliorate the cruelty of the race, to exalt its morals and refine its manners, and to restrain society by stronger bonds than those which human laws impose. Such being their purpose, he who gives a thought to the life of man at large will enter their vanished sanctuaries with sympathy; and if no mystery any longer attaches to what they taught—least of all to their ancient allegory of immortality—there is the abiding interest in the rites, drama, and symbols employed in the teaching of wise and good and beautiful truth.

What influence the Mysteries had on the new, uprising Christianity is hard to know, and the issue is still in debate. That they did influence the early Church is evident from the writings of the Fathers—more than one of whom boasted of initiation—and some go so far as to say that the Mysteries died at last, only to live again in the ritual of the Church.

St. Paul in his missionary journeys came in contact with the Mysteries, and even makes use of some of their technical terms in his Epistles, the better to show that what they sought to teach by drama can be known only by spiritual experience. No doubt his insight is sound, but surely drama may assist to that realization, else public worship might also come under ban.

Of the Eleusinian Mysteries in particular, we have long needed such a study as is here offered, in which the author not only sums up in an attractive manner what is known, but adds to our knowledge some important details. An Egyptian source has been attributed to the Mysteries of Greece, but there is little evidence of it, save as we may conjecture it to have been so, remembering the influence of Egypt upon Greece. Such influences are difficult to trace, and it is safer to say that the idea and use of Initiation—as old as the Men's House of primitive society—was universal, and took different forms in different lands.

Such a study has more than an antiquarian interest, not only to students in general, but especially to the men of the gentle Craft of Freemasonry. If we may not say that Freemasonry is historically descended from the instituted Mysteries of antiquity, it does perpetuate, to some extent, their ministry among us. At least, the resemblance between those ancient rites and the ceremonials of both Operative and Speculative Freemasonry are very striking; and the present study must be reckoned as not the least of the services of its author to that gracious Craft.

THE CITY TEMPLE, LONDON, E.C.

The Eleusinian Mysteries and Rites

I

THE ELEUSINIAN LEGEND

THE legend which formed the basis of the Mysteries of Eleusis, presence at and participation in which demanded an elaborate form or ceremony of initiation, was as follows :—

Persephone (sometimes described as Proserpine and as Cora or Kore), when gathering flowers, was abducted by Pluto, the god of Hades, and carried off by him to his gloomy abode ; Zeus, the brother of Pluto and the father of Persephone, giving his consent. Demeter (or Ceres), her mother, arrived too late to assist her child, or even catch a glimpse of her seducer, and neither god nor man was able, or willing, to enlighten her as to the whereabouts of Persephone or who had carried her away. For nine nights and days she wandered, torch in hand, in quest of her child. Eventually, however, she heard from Helios (the sun) the name of the seducer and his accomplice. Incensed at Zeus, she left Olympos and the gods, and came down to scour the earth disguised as an old woman.

In the course of her wanderings she arrived at Eleusis, where she was honourably entertained by Keleos, the ruler of the country, with whom, and his wife Metanira, she consented to remain in order to watch over the education of Demophon, who had just been born to the aged king and whom she undertook to make immortal.

> Long was thy anxious search
> For lovely Proserpine, nor didst thou break
> Thy mournful fast, till the far-fam'd Eleusis
> Received thee wandering.
>
> *Orphic Hymn.*

The city of Eleusis is said to derive its name from the hero Eleusis, a fabulous personage deemed by some to have been the offspring of Mercury and Daira, daughter of Oceanus, while by others he was claimed as the son of Oxyges.

Unknown to the parents Demeter used to anoint Demophon by day with ambrosia, and hide him by night in the fire like a firebrand. Detected one night by Metanira, she was compelled to reveal herself as Demeter, the goddess. Whereupon she directed the Eleusinians to erect a temple as a peace-offering, and, this being done, she promised to initiate them into the form of worship which would obtain for them her goodwill and favour. "It is I, Demeter, full of glory, who lightens and gladdens the hearts of gods and men. Hasten ye, my people, to raise, hard by the citadel, below the ramparts, a fane, and on the eminence of the hill, an altar, above the wall of Callichorum. I will instruct you in the rites which shall be observed and which are pleasing to me."

The temple was erected, but Demeter was still vowing vengeance against gods and men, and because of the continued loss of her daughter she rendered the earth sterile during a whole year.

> What ails her that she comes not home?
>   Demeter seeks her far and wide;
> And gloomy-browed doth ceaseless roam
>   From many a morn till eventide.
> "My life, immortal though it be,
> Is naught!" she cries, "for want of thee,
>   Persephone—Persephone!"

The oxen drew the plough, but in vain was the seed sown in the prepared ground. Mankind was threatened with utter annihilation, and all the gods were deprived of sacrifices and offerings. Zeus endeavoured to appease the anger of the gods, but in vain. Finally he summoned Hermes to go to Pluto and order him to restore Persephone to her mother. Pluto yielded, but before Persephone left she took from the hand of Pluto four pomegranate pips which he offered her as sustenance on her journey.

Persephone, returning from the land of shadows, found her mother in the temple at Eleusis which had recently been erected. Her first question was whether her daughter had eaten anything in the land of her imprisonment, because her unconditional return to earth and Olympos depended upon that. Persephone informed her mother that all she had eaten was the pomegranate pips, in consequence of which Pluto demanded that Persephone should sojourn with him for four months during each year, or one month for each pip taken. Demeter had no option but to consent to this arrangement, which meant that she would enjoy the company of Persephone for eight months in every year, and that the remaining four would be spent by Persephone with Pluto. Demeter caused to awaken anew "the fruits of the fertile plains," and the whole earth was re-clothed with leaves and flowers. Demeter called together the princes of Eleusis—Triptolemus, Diocles, Eumolpus, Polyxenos, and Keleos—and initiated them "into the sacred rites—most venerable—into which no one is allowed to make enquiries or to divulge; a solemn warning from the gods seals our mouths."

Although secrecy on the subject of the nature of the stately Mysteries is strictly enjoined, the writer of the Homeric Hymn to Demeter makes no secret of the happiness which belonged to all who became initiates: "Happy is he who has been received unfortunate he who has never received the initiation nor taken part in the sacred ordinances, and who cannot, alas! be destined to the same lot reserved for the faithful in the darkling abode."

The earliest mention of the Temple of Demeter at Eleusis occurs in the Homeric Hymn to Demeter, which has already been mentioned. This was not written by Homer, but by some poet versed in Homeric lore, and its probable date is about 600 B.C. It was discovered a little over a hundred years ago in an old monastery library at Moscow, and now reposes in a museum at Leyden.

In this Homeric Hymn to Demeter, Persephone gives her own version of the incident as follows: "We were all playing in the lovely meadows—Leucippe, and Phaino, and Electra, and Ianthe, and Melitê, and Iachê and Rhodeia, and Callinhoe, and Melobosis, and Ianeira, and Acastê, and Admetê, and Rhodope, and Plouto, and winsome Calypso, and Styx, and Urania, and beautiful Galaxamê. We were playing there and plucking beautiful blossoms with our hands; crocuses mingled, and iris, and hyacinth, and roses, and lilies, a marvel to behold, and narcissus, that the wide earth bare, a wile for my undoing. Gladly was I gathering them when the earth gaped beneath, and therefrom leaped the mighty prince, the host of many guests, and he bare me against my will, despite my grief, beneath the earth, in his golden chariot; and shrilly did I cry."

The version of the legend given by Minucius Felix is as follows: "Proserpine, the daughter of Ceres by Jupiter, as she was gathering tender flowers in the new spring, was ravished from her delightful abode by Pluto; and, being carried from thence through thick woods and over a length of sea, was brought by Pluto into a cavern, the residence of departed spirits, over whom she afterwards ruled with absolute sway. But Ceres, upon discovering the loss of her daughter, with lighted torches and begirt with a serpent, wandered over the whole earth for the purpose of finding her, till she came to Eleusis; there she found her daughter, and discovered to the Eleusinians the plantation of corn."

According to another version of the legend, Neptune met Ceres when she was in quest of her daughter, and fell in love with her. The goddess, in order to escape from his attentions, concealed herself under the form of a mare, when the god of the sea transformed himself into a horse to seduce her, with which act she was so highly offended that after having washed herself in a river and reassumed human form, she took refuge in a cave, where she lay concealed. When famine and pestilence began to ravage the earth, the gods made search for her everywhere, but could not find her until Pan discovered her and apprised Jupiter of her whereabouts. This cave was in Sicily, in which country Ceres was known as the black Ceres, or the Erinnys, because the outrages offered her by Neptune turned her frantic and furious. Demeter was depicted in Sicily as clad in black, with a horse's head, holding a pigeon in one hand and a dolphin in the other.

On the submission of Eleusis to Athens, the Mysteries became an integral part of the Athenian religion, so that the Eleusinian Mysteries became a Panhellenic institution, and later, under the Romans, a universal worship, but the secret rites of initiation were well kept throughout their history.

Eleusis was one of the twelve originally independent cities of Attica, which Theseus is said to have united into a simple state. Leusina now occupies the site, and has thus preserved the name of the ancient city.

Theseus is portrayed by Virgil as suffering eternal punishment in Hades, but Proclus writes concerning him as follows: "Theseus, and Pirithous are fabled to have ravished Helen, and to have descended to the infernal regions—i.e. they were lovers of intelligible and visible beauty. Afterwards Theseus was liberated by Pericles from Hades, but Pirithous remained there because he could not sustain the arduous attitude of divine contemplation."

Dr. Warburton, in his *Divine Legation of Moses*, gives it as his opinion that Theseus was a living character who once forced his way into the Eleusinian Mysteries, for which crime he was imprisoned on earth and afterwards damned in the infernal regions.

The Eleusinian Mysteries seem to have constituted the most vital portion of the Attic religion, and always to have retained something of awe and solemnity. They were not known outside Attica until the time of the Median wars, when they spread to the Greek colonies in Asia as part of the constitution of the daughter states, where the cult seems to have exercised a considerable influence both on the populace and on the philosophers. Outside Eleusis the Mysteries were not celebrated so frequently nor on so magnificent a scale. At Celeas, where they were celebrated every fourth year, a hierophant, who was not bound by the law of celibacy, as at Eleusis, was elected by the people for each celebration. Pausanias is the authority for a statement by the Phliasians that they imitated the Eleusinian Mysteries. They maintained, however, that their rendering was instituted by Dysaules, brother of Celeus, who went to their country after he had been expelled from Eleusis by Ion, the son of Xuthus, at the time when Ion was chosen commander-in-chief of the Athenians in the war against Eleusis. Pausanias disputed that any Eleusinian was defeated in battle and forced into exile, maintaining that peace was concluded between the Athenians and the Eleusinians before the war was fought out, even Eumolpus himself being permitted to remain in Eleusis. Pausanias, also, while admitting that Dysaules might have gone to Phlias for some cause other than that admitted by the Phliasians, questioned whether Dysaules was related to Celeus, or, indeed, to any illustrious Eleusinian family. The name of Dysaules does not occur in the Homeric Hymn to Demeter, where are enumerated all who were taught the ritual of the Mysteries by the goddess, though that of Celeus is mentioned :—

> She showed to Triptolemus and Diocles, smiter of horses
> And mighty Eumolpus and Celeus, leader of people,
> The way of performing the sacred rites and explained to all of them the orgies.

Nevertheless, according to the Phliasians, it was Dysaules who instituted the Mysteries among them.

The Pheneatians also had a sanctuary dedicated to Demeter, which they called Eleusinian, and in which they celebrated the Mysteries in honour of the goddess. They had a legend that Demeter went thither in her wanderings, and that, out of gratitude to the Pheneatians for the hospitality they showed her, she gave them all the different kinds of pulse, except beans. Two Pheneatians—Trisaules and Damithales—built a temple to Demeter Thesuria, the goddess of laws, under Mount Cyllene, where were instituted the Mysteries in her honour which were celebrated until a late period, and which were said to be introduced there by Naus, a grandson of Eumolpus.

" Much that is excellent and divine," wrote Cicero, " does Athens seem to me to have produced and added to our life, but nothing better than those Mysteries by which we are formed and moulded from a rude and savage state of humanity; and, indeed, in the Mysteries we perceive the real principles of life, and learn not only to live happily, but to die with a fairer hope." Every manner of writer—religious poet, worldly poet, sceptical philosopher, orator—all are of one mind about this, that the Mysteries were far and away the greatest of all the religious festivals of Greece.

II

THE RITUAL OF THE MYSTERIES

THE Eleusinian Mysteries, observed by nearly all Greeks, but particularly by the Athenians, were celebrated yearly at Eleusis, though in the earlier annals of their history they were celebrated once in every three years only, and once in every four years by the Celeans, Cretans, Parrhasians, Pheneteans, Phliasians, and Spartans. It was the most celebrated of all the religious ceremonies of Greece at any period of the country's history, and was regarded as of such importance that the Festival is referred to frequently simply as "The Mysteries." The rites were guarded most jealously and carefully concealed from the uninitiated. If any person divulged any part of them he was regarded as having offended against the divine law, and by the act he rendered himself liable to divine vengeance. It was accounted unsafe to abide in the same house with him, and as soon as his offence was made public he was apprehended. Similarly, drastic punishment was meted out to any person not initiated into the Mysteries who chanced to be present at their celebration, even through ignorance or genuine error.

The Mysteries were divided into two parts—the Lesser Mysteries and the Greater Mysteries. The Lesser Mysteries were said to have been instituted when Hercules, Castor, and Pollux expressed a desire to be initiated, they happening to be in Athens at the time of the celebration of the Mysteries by the Athenians in accordance with the ordinance of Demeter. Not being Athenians, they were ineligible for the honour of initiation, but the difficulty was overcome by Eumolpus, who was desirous of including in the ranks of the initiated a man of such power and eminence as Hercules, foreigner though he might be. The three were first made citizens, and then as a preliminary to the initiation ceremony as prescribed by the goddess, Eumolpus instituted the Lesser Mysteries, which then and afterwards became a ceremony preliminary to the Greater Mysteries, as they then became known, for candidates of alien birth. In later times this Lesser Festival, celebrated in the month of Anthesterion at the beginning of spring, at Agra, became a general preparation for the Greater Festival, and no persons were initiated into the Greater Mysteries until they had first been initiated into the Lesser.

With regard to Hercules, there is a legend that on a certain time Hercules wished to become a member of one of the secret societies of antiquity.

He accordingly presented himself and applied in due form for initiation. His case was referred to a council of wise and virtuous men, who objected to his admission on account of some crimes which he had committed. Consequently he was rejected. Their words to him were: "You are forbidden to enter here; your heart is cruel, your hands are stained with crime. Go! repair the wrong you have done; repent of your evil doings, and then come with pure heart and clean hands, and the doors of our Mysteries shall be opened to you." The legend goes on to say that after his regeneration he returned and became a worthy member of the Order.

The ceremonies of the Lesser Mysteries were entirely different from those of the Greater Mysteries. The Lesser Mysteries represented the return of Persephone to earth—which, of course, took place at Eleusis; and the Greater Mysteries represented her descent to the infernal regions. The Lesser Mysteries honoured the daughter more than the mother, who was the principal figure in the greater Mysteries. In the Lesser Mysteries, Persephone was known as Pherrephatta, and in the Greater Mysteries she was given the name of Kore. Everything was, in fact, a mystery, and nothing was called by its right name. Lenormant says that it is certain that the initiated of the Lesser Mysteries carried away from Agra a certain store of religious knowledge which enabled them to understand the symbols and representations which were displayed afterwards before their eyes at the Greater Mysteries at Eleusis.

The object of the Lesser Mysteries was to signify occultly the condition of the impure soul invested with a terrene body and merged in a material nature. The Greater Mysteries taught that he who, in the present life, is in subjection to his irrational part, is truly in Hades. If Hades, then, is the region of punishment and misery, the purified soul must reside in the region of bliss, theoretically, in the present life, and according to a deific energy in the next. They intimated by gorgeous mystic visions the felicity of the soul, both here and hereafter, when purified from the defilements of a material nature and consequently elevated to the realities of intellectual vision.

The Mysteries were supposed to represent in a kind of moral drama the rise and establishment of civil society, the doctrine of a state of future rewards and punishments, the errors of polytheism, and the Unity of the Godhead, which last article was afterwards demonstrated to be their famous secret. The ritual was produced from the sanctuary. It was enveloped in symbolical figures of animals which suggested a correspondence which was utterly inexplicable to the uninitiated.

K. O. Müller, in his *History of the Literature of Ancient Greece*, says :—

" All the Greek religious poetry treating of death and the world beyond the grave refers to the deities whose influence was supposed to be exercised in this dark region at the centre of the earth, and were thought to have little connection with the political and social relations of human life. These deities formed a class apart from the gods of Olympus and were comprehended under the name of the Chthenian gods (gods of the underworld). The mysteries of the Greeks were connected with the worship of those gods alone. That a love of immortality first found a support in a belief in these deities appears from the fable of Persephone, the daughter of Demeter. Every year at the time of harvest, Persephone was supposed to be carried from the world above to the dark dominions of the invisible King of Shadows, and to return every spring in youthful beauty to the arms of her mother. It was thus that the ancient Greeks described the disappearance and return of vegetable life in the alternations of the seasons. The changes of Nature, however, must have been considerable in typifying the changes in the lot of man ; otherwise Persephone would have been merely a symbol of the seed committed to the ground and would not have become queen of the dead. But when the goddess of inanimate nature had become queen of the dead, it was a natural analogy, which must have early suggested itself, that the return of Persephone to the world of light also denoted a renovation of life and a new birth in man. Hence the Mysteries of Demeter, and especially those celebrated at Eleusis, inspired the most elevated and animating hopes with regard to the condition of the soul after death."

No one was permitted to attend the Mysteries who had incurred the sentence of capital punishment for treason or conspiracy, but all other exiles were permitted to be present and were not molested in any way during the whole period of the Festival. No one could be arrested for debt during the holding of the Festival.

Scarcely anything is known of the programme observed during the course of the Lesser Mysteries. They were celebrated on the 19th to 21st of the month Anthesterion, and, like the Greater Mysteries, were preceded and followed by a truce on the part of all engaged in warfare. The same officials presided at both celebrations. The Lesser Mysteries opened with a sacrifice to Demeter and Persephone, a portion of the victims offered being reserved for the members of the sacred families of Eumolpus and Keryce. The main object of the Lesser Mysteries was to put the candidates for initiation in a condition of ritual purification, and, according to Clement of Alexandria, they included certain instructions and preparations for the Greater Mysteries. Like the Eleusinian Mysteries, properly so called, they included dramatic representations of the rape of Persephone and the wanderings of Demeter; in addition, according to Stephen Byzantium, to certain Dionysian representations.

Two months before the full moon of the month of Boedromion, sphondophoroi or heralds, selected from the priestly families of the Eumolpides and Keryces, went forth to announce the forthcoming celebration of the Greater Mysteries, and to claim an armistice on the part of all who might be waging war. The truce commenced on the 15th of the month preceding the celebration of the Mysteries and lasted until the 10th day of the month following the celebration. In order to be valid the truce had to be proclaimed in and accepted by each Hellenic city.

All arrangements for the proper celebration of the Mysteries, both Lesser and Greater, were in the hands of the families of Eumolpides and Keryces. These were ancient Eleusinian families, whose origin was traced back to the time when Eleusis was independent of Athens, and the former family survived as a priestly caste down to the latest period of Athenian history. Its member possessed the hereditary and the sole right to the secrets of the Mysteries. Hence the recognition by the State of the exclusive right and privilege of these families to direct the initiations and to provide each a half of the religious staff of the temple. The Eumolpides held so eminent a place in the Mysteries that Cicero mentions them alone, to the exclusion of the Keryces.

Pausanias relates that, following a war between the Eleusinians and the Athenians, when Erectheus, King of Athens, conquered Immaradus, son of Eumolpus, the subdued Eleusinians, in making their submission, stipulated that they should remain custodians of the Mysteries, but in all other respects were to be subject to the Athenians. This tradition is disputed by more modern writers, but it was accepted by the Athenians and acted upon generally, and the right of the two families solely to prepare candidates for initiation was recognized by a decree of the fifth century B.C., the privilege being confirmed afterwards at a convention between the representatives of Eleusis and Athens. The Eumolpides were the descendants of a mythical ancestor, Eumolpus, son of Neptune, who is first mentioned in the time of Pisastrus. On the death of Eumolpus according to one legend, Ceryx, the younger of the sons, was left. But the Keryces claimed that Ceryx was a son of Hermes by Aglamus, daughter of Cecrops, and that he was not a son of Eumolpus.

The members of the family of Eumolpides had the first claim upon the flesh of the sacrificed animals, but they were permitted to give a portion to any one else as a reward or recompense for services rendered. But when a sacrifice was offered to any of the infernal divinities, the whole of it had to be consumed by the fire. Nothing must be left. All religious problems relating to the Mysteries which could not be solved by the known laws were addressed to the Eumolpides, whose decision was final.

The meaning of the name "Eumolpus" is "a good singer," and great importance was attached to the quality of the voice in the selection of the hierophant, the chief officiant at the celebration of the Mysteries and at the ceremony of initiation, and who was selected from the family of the Eumolpides. It was essential that the formulæ disclosed to the initiates at Eleusis should be pronounced with the proper intonation, for otherwise the words would have no efficacy. Correct intonation was of far greater importance than syllabic pronunciation.

An explanation of this is given by Maspero, who says: "The human voice is pre-eminently a magical instrument, without which none of the highest operations of art can be successful: each of its utterances is carried into the region of the invisible and there releases forces of which the general run of people have no idea, either as to their existence or their manifold action. Without doubt, the real value of an evocation lies in its text, or the sequence of the words of which it is composed, and the tone in which it is enunciated. In order to be efficacious, the conjuration should be accompanied by chanting, either an incantation or a song. In order to produce the desired effect the sacramental melody must be chanted without the variation of a single modulation: one false note, one mistake in the measure, the introversion of any two of the sounds of which it is composed, and the intended effect is annulled. This is the reason why all who recite a prayer or formula intended to force the gods to perform certain acts must be of true voice. The result of their effort, whether successful or unsuccessful, will depend upon the exactness of their voice. It was the voice, therefore, which played the most important part in the oblation, in the prayer of definite request, and in the evocation—in a word, in every instance where man sought to seize hold of the god."

Apart from a "true voice" the words were merely dead sounds. The character of the voice plays an important part in many religions. The Vedas contain in them many invocations and hymns which no uninitiated Brahman can recite: it is only the initiate who knows their true properties and how to put them into use. Some of the hymns of the *Rig-Veda,* when anagrammatically arranged, will yield all the secret invocations which were used for magical purposes in the Brahmanical ceremonies. Some Parsees pay much attention to what is called *ázád dwá* or "free voice." It is recorded in Moslem tradition that a revelation came to the venerated Arabian prophet resembling "the tone of a bell." The effects which low, monotonous chanting produce on nervous people and children are well known. Even animals and serpents are amenable to the influence of sound.

The hierophant was a revealer of holy things. He was a citizen of Athens, a man of mature age, and held his office for life, devoting himself wholly to the service of the temple and living a chaste life, to which end it was usual for him to anoint himself with the juice of hemlock, which, by its extreme coldness, was said to extinguish in a great measure the natural heat. In the opinion of some writers celibacy was an indispensable condition of the highest branch of the priesthood; but, according to inscriptions which have been discovered, some at any rate of the hierophants were married, so that, in all probability, the rule was that during the celebration of the Mysteries and, probably, for a certain time before and after, it was incumbent on the hierophant to abstain from all sexual intercourse. Foucart is of opinion that celibacy was demanded only during the celebration of the Mysteries, although Pausanias states definitely otherwise. In support of Foucart it may be stated that among the inscriptions discovered at Eleusis there is one dedicating a statue to a hierophant by his wife. It was essential that the hierophant should be a man of commanding presence and lead a simple life. On being raised to the dignity he received a kind of consecration at a special ceremony, at which only those of his own rank were permitted to be present, when he was entrusted with certain secrets pertaining to his high office. Prior to this ceremony he went through a special purificatory rite, immersing himself in the sea, an act to which the Greeks attributed great virtue. He had to be exemplary in his moral conduct, and was regarded by the people as being particularly holy. The qualifications of a hierophant were so high that the office could not be regarded as hereditary, for it would have been an exception to find both father and son in possession of the many various and high qualifications regarded as essential to the holding of the office. The robe of the hierophant was a long purple garment; his hair, crowned with a wreath of myrtle, flowed in long locks over his shoulders, and a diadem ornamented his forehead. At the celebration of the Mysteries he was held to represent the Creator of the world. He alone was permitted to penetrate into the innermost shrine in the Hall of the Mysteries—the holy of holies, as it were—and then only once during the celebration of the Mysteries, when, at the most solemn moment of the whole mystic celebration, his form appeared suddenly to be transfigured with light before the rapt gaze of the initiated. He alone was permitted to reveal to the fully initiated the mystic objects, the sight of which marked the completion of their admission into the community. He had the power of refusing admission to those applicants whom he deemed unfit to be entrusted with the secrets. He was not inactive during the intervals between the celebrations of the Mysteries. It was his duty to superintend the instruction of the candidates for initiation, who for that purpose were divided into groups and instructed by officials known as mystagogues. The personal name of the hierophant was never mentioned. It was supposed to be unknown, "wafted away into the sea by the mystic law," and he was known only by the title of the office which he bore.

An interesting inscription was found some years ago at Eleusis, engraved on the base of a statue erected to a hierophant: "Ask not my name; the mystic rule (or packet) has carried it away into the blue sea. But when I reach the fated day, and go to the abode of the blest, then all who care for me will pronounce it." One of his sons had written below this inscription, after the death of the hierophant: "Now we, his children, reveal the name of the best of fathers, which, when alive, he hid in the depths of the sea. This is the famous Apollonius." There is extant an epigram by a female hierophant, which runs: "Let my name remain unspoken: on being shut off from the world when the sons of Cecrops made me hierophantide to Demeter, I myself hid it in the vasty depths." Eunapius, in *Vita Maxim*, says: "I may not tell the name of him who was then hierophant, for it was he who initiated me." The manner in which the name was committed to the sea was either by the immersion of the bearer or by writing the name on a leaden tablet, which was cast into the sea. The holy name, by which the hierophant was afterwards known, was derived from the name of some god or bore some ritualistic meaning. Sometimes the hierophant was known simply by the title of his office with the addition of his father's name. The rule as to the public mention of the former name of the hierophant was occasionally transgressed, and there is the instance of the atheistic philosopher Theodorus addressing a hierophant by his discarded name of Lacrateides, and also of Deinias, who was put into prison for the offence of addressing a hierophant by his discarded family name.

Lucian refers to this in one passage in *Lexiphanes*: "The first I met were a torch-bearer, a hierophant, and others of the initiated, haling Deinias before the judge, and protesting that he had called them by their names, though he well knew that, from the time of their sanctification, they were nameless, and no more to be named but by hallowed names."

In the Imperial Inscriptions we find the titles substituted for the proper names.[1] The hierophant

[1] From two inscriptions found at Eleusis it would appear that it was customary to make the name public after the death of the hierophant. It seems also to have been the practice to make the name known to the initiate under the pledge of secrecy. Sir James Frazer thinks that the names were, in all probability, engraved on tablets of bronze or lead and then thrown into deep water in the Gulf of Salamis.

was compelled to avoid contact with the dead in the same manner as the Cohanim of the Jewish faith, and with certain animals reputed to be unclean. Contact with any person from whom blood was issuing also caused impurity. He was assisted by a female hierophant, or hierophantide—an attendant upon the goddess Demeter and her daughter Persephone. She also was selected from the family of the Eumolpides and was chosen for life. She was permitted to marry, and several inscriptions mention the names of children of hierophantides. On her initiation into this high degree she was brought forward naked to the side of a sacred font, in which her right hand was placed, the priest declaring her to be true and holy and dedicated to the service of the temple. The special duty of the female hierophant was to superintend the initiation of female aspirants, but she was present throughout the ceremony and played some part in the initiation of the male candidates. An inscription on the tomb of one hierophantide mentions to her glory that she had set the myrtle crown, the seal of mystic communion, on the heads of the illustrious initiates, Marcus Aurelius and his son, Commodus. Another gloried in the fact that she had initiated the Emperor Hadrian.

Next in rank to the hierophant and hierophantide came the male and female dadouchos, who were taken from the family of the Keryces. They were the torch-bearers, and their duty consisted mainly in carrying the torches at the Sacred Festival. They also wore purple robes, myrtle crowns, and diadems. They were appointed for life, and were permitted to marry. The male dadouchos particularly was associated with the hierophant in certain solemn and public functions, such as the opening address to the candidates for initiation and in the public prayers for the welfare of the State. The office was frequently handed down from father to son. Until the first century B.C. the dadouchos was never addressed by his own personal name, but always by the title of his office.

The hierocceryx, or messenger of holy tidings, was the representative of Hermes, or Mercury, who, as the messenger of the gods, was indispensable as mediator whenever men wished to approach the Immortals. He also wore a purple-coloured robe and a myrtle crown. He was chosen for life from the family of the Keryces. He made the necessary proclamations to the candidates for initiation into the various degrees, and in particular enjoined them to preserve silence. It was necessary for him to have passed through all the various degrees, as his duties necessitated his presence throughout the ceremonial.

The phaidantes had the custody of the sacred statues and the sacred vessels, which they had to maintain in good repair. They were selected from one or other of the two sacerdotal families.

Among the other officials were: The liknophori, who carried the mystic fan; the hydranoi, who purified the candidates for initiation by sprinkling them with holy water at the commencement of the Festival; the spondophoroi, who proclaimed the sacred truce, which was to permit of the peaceful celebration of the Mysteries; the pyrphoroi, who brought and maintained the fire for the sacrifices; the hieraules, who played the flute during the time the sacrifices were being offered—they were the leaders of the sacred music, who had under their charge the hymnodoi, the hymnetriai; the neokoroi, who maintained the temples and the altars; the panageis, who formed a class between the ministers and the initiated. Then there were the "initiates of the altar," who performed expiatory rites in the name and in the place of all the initiated. There were also many other minor officials, by the general name of melissæ—i.e. bees, perhaps so-called because bees, being makers of honey, were sacred to Demeter. The diluvian priestesses and regenerated souls were called "bees." All these officials had to be of unblemished reputation, and wore myrtle crowns while engaged in the service of the temple.

The officials; whose duty it was to take care that the ritual was punctiliously followed in every detail, included nine archons, who were chosen every year to manage the affairs of Greece. The first of these was always the King, or Archon Basileus, whose duty at the celebration of the Mysteries it was to offer prayers and sacrifices, to see that no indecency or irregularity was committed during the Festival, and at the conclusion to pass judgment on all offenders. There were also four epimeletæ, or curators, elected by the people, one being appointed from the Eumolpides, another from the Keryces, and the remaining two from the rank and file of the citizens; and ten hieropoioi, whose duty it was to offer sacrifices. It may be worthy of remark here that Epimenides of Crete, who flourished about the year 600 B.C., is said by Diogenes Laertius, in his life of that philosopher, to have been the first to perform expiatory sacrifices and lustrations in fields and houses and to have been the first to erect temples for the purpose of sacrifice.

The sacred symbols used in the ceremonies were enclosed in a special chamber in the Telestrion, or Hall of Initiation, known as the Anactoron, into which the hierophant alone had the right to penetrate. During the celebration of the Mysteries they were carried to Athens veiled and hidden from the gaze of the profane, whence they were taken back to Eleusis. It was permitted only to the initiated to look upon these "hiera," as they were called. These sacred objects were in the charge of the Eumolpides family.

Written descriptions, however graphic or eloquent, convey but a faint impression of the wonderful scenes that were enacted; Aristides says that what was seen rivalled anything that was heard. Another writer has declared: "Many a wondrous sight may be seen and not a few tales of wonder may be heard in Greece; but there is nothing on which the blessing of God rests in so full a measure as the rites of Eleusis and the Olympic games." For nine centuries—that period of time being divided almost equally between the pre-Christian and Christian eras—they were the Palladium of Greek Paganism. In the latter part of their history, when the restrictions as to admission began to be relaxed, and in proportion to that relaxation, their essential religious character disappeared, they became but a ceremony, their splendour being their principal attraction, until finally they degenerated into a mere superstition. Julian strived in vain to infuse new life into the vanishing cult, but it was too late—the Eleusinian Mysteries were dead.

The Athenians were pious in the extreme, and throughout the period that initiation was limited to that race the reputation of Eleusis was maintained, although pilgrims from various and remote parts of the world visited it at the season of the Mysteries. When the Eleusinian Mysteries were taken to Rome, as they were in the reign of Hadrian, they contracted impurities and degenerated into riot and vice; the spirituality of their teachings did not accompany the transference or it failed to be comprehended

Although the forms of initiation were still symbolical of the original and noble objects of the institution, the licentious Romans mistook the shadow for the substance, and while they passed through all the ceremonies they were strangers to the objects for which they were framed.

In A.D. 364, a law prohibiting nocturnal rites was published by Valentinian, but Praetextatus, whom Julian had constituted governor of Achaia, prevailed on him to revoke it, urging that the lives of the Greeks would be rendered utterly unsupportable if he deprived them of this, their most holy and comprehensive festival. Much has been made by some writers of the fact that the ceremonies were held at night, but in the early days of Christianity also it was the custom for Christians to forgather either at night or before daybreak, a circumstance which led to their assemblies being known as *antelucani* and themselves as *lucifugæ* or "light-haters," by way of reproach. About the beginning of the fifth century Theodosius the Great prohibited and almost totally extinguished the pagan theology in the Roman Empire, and the Eleusinian Mysteries suffered in the general destruction. It is probable, however, that the Mysteries were celebrated secretly in spite of the severe edicts of Theodosius and that they were partly continued through the dark ages, though stripped of their splendour. It is certain that many rites of the pagan religion were performed under the dissembled name of convivial meetings, long after the publication of the Emperor's edicts, and Psellius informs us that the Mysteries of Ceres existed in Athens until the eighth century of the Christian era and were never totally suppressed.

The Festival of the Greater Mysteries—and this was, of course, by far the more important—began on the 15th of the month of Boedromion, corresponding roughly with the month of September, and lasted until the 23rd of the same month. During that time it was unlawful to arrest any man present, or present any petition except for offences committed at the Festival, heavy penalties being inflicted for breaches of this law, the penalties fixed being a fine of not less than a thousand drachmas, and some assert that transgressors were even put to death.

III

PROGRAMME OF THE GREATER MYSTERIES

THE following is the programme of the "Greater Mysteries," which extended over a period of ten days. The various functions were characterized by the greatest possible solemnity and decorum, and the ceremonies were regarded as "religious" in the highest interpretation of that term.

FIRST DAY.—The first day was known as the "Gathering," or the "Assembly," when all who had passed through the Lesser Mysteries assembled to assist in the celebration of the Greater Mysteries. On this day the Archon Basileus presided over all the cults of the city, and assembled the people at a place known as the Poikile Stoa. After the Archon Basileus, with four assistants, had offered up sacrifices and prayers for the welfare of Greece, the following proclamation was made by the Archon Basileus, wearing his robe of office :—

"Come, whoever is clean of all pollution and whose soul has not consciousness of sin. Come, whosoever hath lived a life of righteousness and justice. Come all ye who are pure of heart and of hand, and whose speech can be understood. Whosoever hath not clean hands, a pure soul, and an intelligible voice must not assist at the Mysteries."

The people were then commanded by the hierophant to wash their hands in consecrated water, and the impious were threatened with the punishment set forth in the law if they were discovered, but especially, and this in any case, with the implacable anger of the gods. The hierocceryx then impressed upon all the duty of observing the most rigid secrecy with respect to what they might witness, and bade them to be silent throughout the ceremonies, and not utter even an exclamation. The candidates for initiation assembled outside the temple, each under the guidance and direction of the mystagogue, who repeated these instructions to the candidates. Once within the sacred enclosure all the initiates were subject to a purification by fire ceremonial. All wore regalia special to the occasion. This is evident from the wording of inscriptions which have been discovered, but particulars of the regalia are wanting. We know that extravagant and costly dresses were regarded by Demeter with disfavour, and that it was forbidden to wear such in the temple. Jewellery, gold ornaments, purple-coloured belts, and embroideries were also barred, as were robes and cloths of mixed colours. The hair of women had to fall down loose upon the shoulders, and must not be in plaits or coiled upon the head. No woman was permitted to use cosmetics.

SECOND DAY.—The second day was known as *Halade Mystæ*, or "To the sea, ye mystæ," from the command which greeted all the initiates to go and purify themselves by washing in the sea, or in the salt water of the two consecrated lakes, called Rheiti, on what was known as "The Sacred Way." The priests had the exclusive right of fishing in these lakes. A procession was formed, in which all joined and made their way to the sea or the lakes, where they bathed and purified themselves. This general purification was akin to that practised to this day by the Jews at the beginning of the Jewish year. The day was consecrated to Saturn, into whose province the soul is said to fall in the course of its descent from the tropic of Cancer. Capella compares Saturn to a river, voluminous, sluggish, and cold. The planet signifies pure intellect, and Pythagoras symbolically called the sea a tear of Saturn. The bathing was preceded by a confession, and the manner in which the bathing was carried out and the number of immersions varied with the degree of guilt which each confessed. According to Suidas, those who had to purify themselves from murder plunged into salt water on two separate occasions, immersing themselves seven times on each occasion. On returning from the bath all were regarded as "new creatures," the bath being regarded as a laver of regeneration, and the initiates were clothed in a plain fawn-skin or a sheep-skin. The purification, however, was not regarded as complete until the following day, when there was added the sprinkling of the blood of a pig sacrificed. Each had carried to the river or lake a little pig, which was also purified by bathing, and on the next day this pig was sacrificed. The pig was offered because it was very pernicious to cornfields. On the Eleusinian coinage the pig, standing on a torch placed horizontally, appears as the sign and symbol of the Mysteries. On this day also some of the initiated submitted to a special purification near the altar of Zeus Mellichios on the Sacred Way. For each person whom it was desired to purify an ox was sacrificed to Zeus Mellichios, the infernal Zeus, the skin of the animal was laid on the ground by the dadouchos, and the one who was the object of the lustration remained there squatting on the left foot.

THIRD DAY.—On the third day pleasures of every description, even the most innocent, were strictly forbidden, and every one fasted till nightfall, when they partook of seed cakes, parched corn, salt, pomegranates, and sacred wine mixed with milk and honey. The Archon Basileus, assisted again by the four epimeletæ, celebrated, in the presence of representatives from the allied cities, the great sacrifice of the Soteria for the well-being of the State, the Athenian citizens, and their wives and children. This ceremony took place in the Eleusinion at the foot of the Acropolis. The day was known as the Day of Mourning, and was supposed to commemorate Demeter's grief at the loss of Persephone. The sacrifices offered consisted chiefly of a mullet and of barley out of Rharium, a field of Eleusis. The oblations were accounted so sacred that the priests themselves were not permitted, as was usual in other offerings, to partake of them. At the conclusion of the general ceremony each one individually sacrificed the little pig purified in the sea the night before.

The hog of propitiation offered to Frey was a solemn sacrifice in the North of Europe and in Sweden, down to modern times, the custom has been preserved by baking, on Christmas Eve, a loaf or cake in the form of a hog.

Fourth Day.—The principal event of the fourth day was a solemn procession, when the holy basket of Ceres (Demeter) was carried in a consecrated cart, the crowds of people shouting as it went along, "Hail, Ceres!" The rear end of the procession was composed of women carrying baskets containing sesamin, carded wool, grains of salt, corn, pomegranates, reeds, ivy boughs, cakes known as poppies, and sometimes serpents. One kind of these cakes was known as "ox-cakes"; they were made with little horns and dedicated to the moon. Another kind contained poppy seeds. Poppy was used in the ceremonies because it was said that some grains of poppy were given to Demeter upon her arrival in Greece to induce sleep, which she had not enjoyed from the time of the abduction of Persephone. Demeter is invariably represented in her statues as being very rotund, crowned with ears of corn, and holding in her hand a branch of poppy.

FIFTH DAY.—The fifth day was known as the Day of Torches, from the fact that at nightfall all the initiates walked in pairs round the temple of Demete at Eleusis, the dadouchos himself leading the procession. The torches were waved about and changed from hand to hand, to represent the wanderings of the goddess in search of her daughter when she was conducted by the light of a torch kindled in the flames of Etna.

SIXTH DAY.—Iacchos was the name given to the sixth day of the Festival. The "fair young god," Iacchos, or Dionysos, or Bacchus, was the son of Jupiter and Ceres, and accompanied the goddess in her search for Persephone. He also carried a torch, hence his statue has always a torch in the hand. This statue, together with other sacred objects, were taken from the Iacchion, the sanctuary of Iacchos in Athens, mounted on a heavy rustic four-wheeled chariot drawn by bulls, and, accompanied by the Iacchogogue and other magistrates nominated for the occasion, conveyed from the Kerameikos, or Potter's Quarter, to Eleusis by the Sacred Way in solemn procession. It was on this day that the solemnity of the ceremonial reached its height. The statue, as well as the people accompanying it, were crowned with myrtle, the people dancing all the way along the route, beating brass kettles and playing instruments of various kinds and singing sacred songs. Halts were made during the procession at various shrines, at the site of the house of Phytalus, who, it was said, received the goddess into his house, and, according to an inscription on his tomb, she requited him by revealing to him the culture of the fig; particularly at a fig-tree which was regarded as sacred, because it had the renown of being planted by Phytalus; also upon a bridge built over the river Cephissus, by the side of which Pluto descended into Hades with Persephone, where the bystanders made themselves merry at the expense of the pilgrims. At each of the shrines sacrifices and libations were offered, hymns sung, and sacred dances performed. Having passed the bridge, the people entered Eleusis by what was known as the Mystical Entrance. Midnight had set in before Eleusis was reached, so that a great part of the journey had to be accomplished by the light of the torches carried by each of the pilgrims, and the nocturnal journey was spoken of as the "Night of Torches" by many ancient authors. The pitch and resin of which the torches were composed were substances supposed to have the virtue of warding off evil spirits. The barren mountains of the Pass of Daphni and the surface of the sea resounded with the chant, "Iacchos, O Iacchos!" At one of the halts the Croconians, descendants of the hero Crocon, who had formerly reigned over the Thriasian Plain, fastened a saffron band on the right arm and left foot of each one in the procession. Iacchos was always regarded as a child of Demeter, inasmuch as the vine grows out of the earth. Various symbols were carried by the people, who numbered sometimes as many as from thirty to forty thousand. These symbols consisted of winnowing fans—the "Mystic Fan of Iacchos," plaited reeds and baskets, both relating to the worship of the goddess and her son. The fan, or van, as it was sometimes called, was the instrument that separates the wheat from the chaff, and was regarded also as an emblem of the power which separates the virtuous from the wicked. In the ancient paintings by Bellori two persons are represented as standing by the side of the initiate. One is the priest who is performing the ceremony, who is represented as in a devout posture, and wearing a veil, the old mark of devotion, while another is holding a fan over the head of the candidate. In some of the editions of Southey's translation of the *Æneid* the following lines appear:—

Now learn what arms industrious peasants wield
To sow the furrow's glebe, and clothe the field:

The share, the crooked plough's strong beam, the wain
That slowly rolls on Ceres to her fane:
Hails, sleds, light osiers, and the harrow's load,
The hurdle, and *the mystic van of God.*

The distance covered by the procession was twenty-two kilometres, but Lycurgus ordered that if any woman should ride in a chariot to Eleusis she should be mulcted in a fine of 8,000 drachmas. This was to prevent the richer women from distinguishing themselves from their poorer sisters. Strange to relate, the wife of Lycurgus was the first to break this law, and Lycurgus himself had to pay the fine which he had ordained. He not only paid the penalty, but gave a talent to the informer. Immediately upon the deposit of the sacred objects in the Eleusinion, at the foot of the Acropolis, one of the Eleusinian priests solemnly announced their arrival to the priestess of the tutelary goddess of Athens—Pallas Athene. Plutarch, in commenting upon lucky and unlucky days, says that he is aware that unlucky things happen sometimes on lucky days, for the Athenians had to receive a Macedonian garrison "even on the 20th of Boedromion, the day on which they led forth the mystic Iacchos."

SEVENTH DAY.—On the seventh day the statue was carried back to Athens. The return journey was also a solemn procession, and attended with numerous ceremonies. Halts were again made at several places, like the " stations " of Roman Catholic pilgrimages, when the inhabitants also fell temporarily into line with the procession. For those who remained behind at Eleusis the time was devoted to sports, the combatants appearing naked, and the victors were rewarded with a measure of barley, it being a tradition that that grain was first sown in Eleusis. It was also regarded as a day of solemn preparation by those who were to be initiated on the following night. The return journey was conducted with the same splendour as the outward journey. It comprised comic incidents, the same as on the previous day. Those who awaited the procession at the bridge over the Athenian river Cephisson exchanged all kinds of chaff and buffoonery with those who were in the procession, indulging in what was termed "bridge fooling." These jests, it is said, were to recall the tactful measures employed by a maidservant named Iambe to rouse Demeter from her prolonged sorrowing. There is a strange contradiction in the various statements made by the ancient writers as to what was permissible and what was forbidden during the ceremonies. Demeter, when in search of her daughter, broke down with fatigue at Eleusis, where she sat down on a well, overwhelmed with grief. It was strictly forbidden to any of the initiated to sit down on this well lest it should appear that they were mimicking the weeping goddess. Yet the mimicking of the jests of Iambe were part of the ceremonial of the

Mysteries. According to the ancient writers the "jests," so-called, would be regarded to-day as in bad taste.

> Having thus spoken, she drew aside her garments
> And showed all that shape of the body which it is improper to name—the growth of puberty.
> And with her own hand Iambe stripped herself under the breasts.
> Blandly then the goddess laughed and laughed in her mind,
> And received the glancing cup in which was the draught.

During the Peloponnesian war the Athenians were unable to obtain an armistice from the Lacedæmonians who held Decelea, and it became necessary to send the statue of Iacchos and the processionists to Eleusis by sea. Plutarch says: "Under these conditions it was necessary to omit the sacrifices usually offered all along the road during the passing of Iacchos."

Eighth Day.—The eighth day was called Epidaurion, because it happened once that Æsculapius, coming from Epidaurius to Athens, desired to be initiated, and had the Lesser Mysteries repeated for that purpose. It therefore became customary to celebrate the Lesser Mysteries a second time upon this day, and to admit to initiation any such approved candidates who had not already enjoyed the privilege. There was also another reason for the repetition of the initiatory rites then. The eighth day was regarded as symbolical of the soul falling into the lunar orbi, and the repeated initiation, the second celebration of that sacred rite, was symbolical of the soul bidding adieu to everything of a celestial nature, sinking into a perfect oblivion of her divine origin and pristine felicity, and rushing profoundly into the region of dissimilitude, ignorance, and error. The day opened with a solemn sacrifice offered to Demeter and Persephone, which took place within the peribolus. The utmost precision had to be observed in offering this sacrifice as regarding the age, colour, and sex of the victim, the chants, perfumes, and libations. The acceptance or rejection of a sacrifice was indicated by the movements of the animal as it approached the altar, the vivacity of the flame, the direction of the smoke, etc. If these signs were not favourable in the case of the first victim offered, other animals must be slain until one presented itself in which all the signs were favourable. The flesh of the animal offered was not allowed to be taken outside the sacred precincts, but had to be consumed within the building. The following is said to have been an Invocation used during the celebration of the Mysteries :—

Daughter of Jove, Persephone divine,
Come, blessed queen, and to these rites incline;
Only-begotten, Pluto's honoured wife,
O venerable goddess, source of life:

'Tis thine in earth's profoundities to dwell,
Fast by the wide and dismal gates of hell.
Jove's holy offering, of a beauteous mien,
Avenging goddess, subterranean queen.
The Furies' source, fair-hair'd, whose frame proceeds
From Jove's ineffable and secret seeds.
Mother of Bacchus, sonorous, divine,
And many form'd, the parent of the vine.
Associate of the Seasons, essence bright,
All-ruling virgin, bearing heav'nly light.
With fruits abounding, of a bounteous mind,
Horn'd, and alone desir'd by those of mortal kind.
O vernal queen, whom grassy plains delight,
Sweet to the smell, and pleasing to the sight:
Whose holy forms in budding fruits we view,
Earth's vig'rous offspring of a various hue:
Espous'd in autumn, life and death alone
To wretched mortals from thy pow'r is known:
For thine the task, according to thy will,
Life to produce, and all that lives to kill.
Hear, blessed Goddess, send a rich increase
Of various fruits from earth, with lovely Peace;
Send Health with gentle hand, and crown my life
With blest abundance, free from noisy strife;
Last in extreme old age the prey of death,
Dismiss me willing to the realms beneath,
To thy fair palace and the blissful plains
Where happy spirits dwell, and Pluto reigns.

NINTH DAY.—The ninth day was known as the Day of Earthen Vessels, because it was the custom on that day to fill two jugs with wine. One was placed towards the East and the other towards the West, and after the repetition of certain mystical formulæ both were overthrown, the wine being spilt upon the ground as a libation. The first of these formulæ was directed towards the sky as a prayer for rain, and the second to the earth as a prayer for fertility.

The words used by the hierophant to denote the termination of the celebration of the Mysteries—*Conx Om Pax*: "Watch and do no evil"—are said to have been Egyptian, and were the same as those used at the conclusion of the Mysteries of Isis. This fact is sometimes used as an argument in favour of the Egyptian origin of the Eleusinian Mysteries.

TENTH DAY.—On the tenth day the majority of the people returned to their homes, with the exception of every third and fifth year, when they remained behind for the Mystery Plays and Sports, which lasted from two to three days.

The Eleusinian Games are described by the rhetorician Aristides as the oldest of all Greek games. They are supposed to have been instituted as a thank-offering to Demeter and Persephone at the conclusion of the corn harvest. From an inscription dating from the latter part of the third century B.C. sacrifices were offered to Demeter and Persephone at these games. They included athletic and musical contests, a horse race, and a competition which bore the name of the Ancestral or the Hereditary Contest, the nature of which is not known, but which it is thought may have had its origin in a contest between the reapers on the sacred Rharian plain to see which should first complete his allotted task.

The ancient sanctuary in which the Mysteries were celebrated was burnt by the Persians in 480 or 479 B.C., and a new sanctuary was built—or, at least, begun—under the administration of Pericles. Plutarch says that Corœbus began the Temple of Initiation at Eleusis, but only lived to finish the lower rank of columns with their architraves; Metagenes, of the ward of Xypete, added the rest of the entablature and the upper row of columns, and that Xenocles of Cholargus built the dome on the top. The long wall, the building of which Socrates says he heard Pericles propose to the people, was undertaken by Callicrates. Cratinus satirized the work as proceeding very slowly:—

> Stone upon stone the orator has pil'd
> With swelling words, but words will build no walls.

According to some writers the Temple was planned by Tetinus, the architect of the Parthenon, and Pericles was merely the overseer of the building. We are told by Vitruvius that the Temple at Eleusis consisted at first of one cell of vast magnitude, without columns, though it was probable that it was meant to be surrounded in the customary manner; a prostyle, however, only was added, and that not until the time of Demetrius Phalereus, some ages after the original structure was erected. It is probable that the uncommon magnitude of the cell, added to the various and complicated rites of initiation to the Eleusinian Mysteries, of which it was the scene, prevented its being a peristyle, the expense of which would have been enormous. The Temple was one of the largest of the sacred edifices of Greece. Its length was 68 metres, its breadth 54·66 metres and its superficial area 3716·88 square metres. The monumental altar of sacrifice was placed in front of the façade, close by the eastern angle of the enclosure. According to Virgil the words "Far hence, O be ye far hence, ye profane ones," were inscribed over the main portal.

In the fourth century of the Christian era the Temple of Eleusis was destroyed by the Goths, at the instigation of the monks, who followed the hosts of Alaric.

The revenues from the celebrations must have been considerable. At both the Lesser Mysteries and the Greater Mysteries a charge of one obole a day was demanded from each one attending, which was given to the hierophant. The hierocceryx received a half-obole a day, and other assistants a similar sum. In current coinage an obole was of the value of a fraction over 1¼d.

IV

THE INITIATORY RITES

TWO important facts must be set down with regard to the Mysteries: first, the general custom of all Athenian citizens, and afterwards of all Greeks generally, and eventually of many foreigners, to seek admission into the Eleusinian Mysteries in the only possible manner—viz. by initiation; and, second, the scrupulous care exercised by the Eumolpides to ensure that only persons duly qualified, of irreproachable—or, at any rate, of circumspect, character passed the portals. In the earlier days of the Mysteries it was a necessary condition that the candidates for initiation should be free-born Athenians, but in course of time this rule was relaxed, until eventually strangers (as residents outside Athens were called), aliens, slaves, and even courtesans, were admitted, on condition that they were introduced by a mystagogue, who was, of course, an Athenian. An interesting inscription was discovered a few years ago demonstrating the fact that the public slaves of the city were initiated at the public expense. From historical records we learn that Lysias was enabled without difficulty to secure the initiation of his mistress, Metanira, who was then in the service of the courtesan Nicareta. There always prevailed, however, the strict rule that no one could be admitted who had been guilty of murder or homicide, wilful or accidental, or who had been convicted of witchcraft, and all who had incurred the capital penalty for conspiracy or treason were also excluded. Nero sought admission into the Eleusinian Mysteries, but was rejected because of the many slaughters connected with his name. Antoninus, when he would purge himself before the world of the death of Avidius Cassius, elected to be initiated into the Eleusinian Mysteries, it being recognized at that time that none was admitted into them who was justly guilty of heinous immorality or crime.

Apollonius of Tyana was desirous of being admitted into the Eleusinian Mysteries, but the hierophant refused to admit him on the ground that he was a magician, and had intercourse with divinities other than those of the Mysteries, declaring that he would never initiate a wizard or throw open the Mysteries to a man addicted to impure rites. Apollonius retorted: "You have not yet mentioned the chief of my offences, which is that, knowing, as I do, more about the initiatory rites than you do yourself, I have nevertheless come to you as if you were wiser than I am." The hierophant, when he saw that the exclusion of Apollonius was not by any means popular with the crowd, changed his tone and said: "Be thou initiated, for thou seemest to be some wise man that has come here." But Apollonius replied: "I will be initiated at another time, and it is (mentioning a name) who will initiate me." Hereon, says Philostratus, he showed his gift of prevision, for he glanced at the one who succeeded the hierophant he addressed, and presided over the temple four years later when Apollonius was initiated.

Persons of both sexes and of all ages were initiated, and neglect of the ceremony came to be regarded almost in the light of a crime. Socrates and Demonax were reproached and looked upon with suspicion because they did not apply for initiation. Persians were always pointedly excluded from the ceremony. Athenians of both sexes were granted the privilege of initiation during childhood on the presentation of their father, but only the first degree of initiation was permitted. For the second and third degrees it was necessary to have arrived at full age. The Greeks looked upon initiation in much the same light as the majority of Christians look upon baptism. So great was the rush of candidates for initiation when the restrictions were relaxed that Cicero was able to write that the inhabitants of the most distant regions flocked to Eleusis in order to be initiated. Thus it became the custom with all Romans, who journeyed to Athens to take advantage of the opportunity to become initiates. Even the Emperors of Rome, the official heads of the Roman religion, the masters of the world, came to the Eumolpides to proffer the request that they might receive the honour of initiation and become participants in the Sacred Mysteries revealed by the goddess.

While Augustus, who was initiated in the year 21 B.C., did not hesitate to show his antipathy towards the religion of the Egyptians, towards Judaism and Druidism, he was always scrupulous in observing the pledge of secrecy demanded of initiates into the Eleusinian Mysteries, and on one occasion, when it became necessary for some of the priests of the Eleusinian temple to proceed to Rome to plead before his tribunal on the question of privilege, and in the course of the evidence to speak of certain ceremonial in connection with the Mysteries of which it was not lawful to speak in the presence of the uninitiated, he ordered every one who had not received the privilege of initiation to leave the tribunal so that he and the witnesses alone remained. The Eleusinian Mysteries were not deemed inimical to the welfare of the Roman Empire as were the religions of the Egyptians, Jews, and ancient Britons.

Claudius, another imperial initiate, conceived the idea of transferring the scene of the Mysteries to Rome, and, according to Suetonius, was about to put the project into execution, when it was ruled that it was obligatory that the principal scenic presentation of the Mysteries must be celebrated on the ground trodden by the feet of Demeter and where the goddess herself had ordered her temple to be erected.

The initiation of the Emperor Hadrian (who succeeded where Claudius had failed, in introducing the celebration of the Mysteries into Rome) took place in A.D. 125, when he was present at the Lesser Mysteries in the spring and at the Greater Mysteries in the following autumn. In September, A.D. 129, he was again at Athens, when he presented himself for the third degree, as is known from Dion Cassius, confirmed by a letter written by the Emperor himself, in which he mentions a journey from Eleusis to Ephesus made by him at that time. Hadrian is the only imperial initiate, so far as is known, who persevered and passed through all three degrees. Since he remained at Eleusis as long as it was possible for him to do so after the completion of his initiation, it is not rash to assume that he was inspired by something more than curiosity or even by a desire to show respect.

It is uncertain whether the Emperor Antonin was initiated, although from an inscription it seems probable that he was and that he should be included in the list of imperial initiates. Both Marcus Aurelius and Commodus, father and son, were initiated at the same time, at the Lesser Mysteries in March, A.D. 176, and at the Greater Mysteries in the following September. Septimius Severus was initiated before he ascended the throne.

There was, as stated, three degrees, and the ordinary procedure with regard to initiation was as follows :—

In the month of Anthesterion, the flower month of spring, corresponding with February-March, an applicant could, if approved, become an initiate into the first degree at the celebration of the Lesser Mysteries and take part in their celebration at the Eleusinion at Agra, near to Athens. The ceremony of initiation into this first degree was on a far less imposing scale than the ceremony of initiation into the second and third degrees at the Greater Mysteries. The candidate, however, had to keep chaste and unpolluted for nine days prior to the ceremony, which each one attended wearing crowns and garlands of flowers and observed by offering prayers and sacrifices. Immediately previous to the celebration the candidates for initiation were prepared by the Mystagogues, the special teachers selected for the purpose from the families of the Eumolpides and Keryces. They were instructed in the story of Demeter and Persephone, the character of the purification necessary and other preliminary rites, the fast days, with particulars of the food permissible and forbidden to be eaten, and the various sacrifices to be offered by and for them under the direction of the mystagogues.

Without this preparation no one could be admitted to the Mysteries. There was, however, neither secret doctrine nor dogmatic teaching in this preliminary instruction. Revelation came through contemplation of the sacred objects displayed during the ceremonies by the hierophant, the meaning of which was communicated by means of the mystic formulæ; but the preparation demanded of the initiates, the secrecy imposed, the ceremonies at which the initiates assisted, all of which were performed in the dead of night, created a strong impression and lively hope in regard to the future life. No other cult in Greece, still less the cold Roman religion, had anything of the kind, or approaching to it, to offer. Fasting from food and drink for a certain period before and after initiation was essential, but the candidates did not attach to this act any idea of maceration or expiation of faults: it was simply the reproduction of an event in the life of the goddess, and undergone in order that the body might become more pure. Bowls or vases of consecrated or holy water were placed at the entrance of the temple for the purposes of aspersion. In cases of special or particular impurity an extra preparation extending over two or three days longer became necessary, and unctions of oil or repeated immersions in water were administered. The outward physical purity, the result of immersion prior to initiation, was but the symbol of the inward purity which was supposed to result from initiation. One of the duties of the mystagogues was to see that the candidates were in a state of physical cleanliness both before and throughout the ceremony. According to inscriptions which have been discovered there appear to have been temples or buildings set apart for the cleansing of candidates from special impurities. Initiation into the Lesser Mysteries only permitted the neophyte to go as far as the outer vestibule of the temple.

In the following autumn, if of full age and approved by the hierophant, the neophyte could be initiated into the Greater Mysteries, into the second degree, that of Mysta. This, however, did not secure admission to all the ceremonies performed during the celebration of the Greater Mysteries. A further year, at least, had to elapse before the third degree, that of Epopta, was taken, before he could see with his own eyes and hear with his own ears, all that took place in the temple during the celebration of the Mysteries. Even then, there was one part of the temple and one portion of the ceremony which could be entered and witnessed only by the hierophant and hierophantide.

According to Plutarch, Demetrius, when he was returning to Athens, wrote to the republic that on his arrival he intended to be initiated and to be admitted immediately, not only to the Lesser Mysteries, but to the Greater as well. This was unlawful and unprecedented, though when the letter was read, Pythodorus, a torch-bearer, was the only person who ventured to oppose the demand, and his opposition was entirely ineffectual. Stratocles procured a decree that the month of Munychion should be reputed to be and called the month of Anthesterion, to give Demetrius the opportunity for the initiation into the first degree. This was done, whereupon a second decree was issued by which Munychion was again changed into Boedromion, and Demetrius was admitted to the Mysteries of the next degree. Philippides, the poet, satirized Stratocles in the words: "The man who can contract the whole year into one month," and Demetrius, with reference to his lodging in the Parthenon, in the words: "The man who turns the temples into inns and brings prostitutes into the company of the virgin goddess."

The design of initiation, according to Plato, was to restore the soul to that state from which it fell, and Proclus states that initiation into the Mysteries drew the souls of men from a material, sensual, and merely human life and joined them in communion with the gods. "Happy is the man," wrote Euripides, "who hath been initiated into the Greater Mysteries and leads a life of piety and religion," and Aristophanes truly represented public opinion when he wrote in *The Frogs*: "On us only does the sun dispense his blessings; we only receive pleasure from his beams; we, who are initiated, and perform towards citizens and strangers all acts of piety and justice." The initiates sought to imitate the allegorical birth of the god. The epoptæ were supposed to have experienced a certain regeneration and to enter upon a new state of existence, and they were fantastically deemed to have acquired a great increase of light and knowledge. Hitherto they had been exoteric and profane; now they had become esoteric and holy.

Jevons, in his *Introduction to the Study of Religion*, says that no oath was demanded of the initiate, but that silence was observed generally as an act of reverence rather than as an act of purposed concealment. There seems, however, to be conclusive evidence that an oath of secrecy was demanded of and taken by the candidates for initiation, at any rate, into the second and third degrees, if not into the first degree. Moreover, there are on record several prosecutions of citizens for having broken the pledge of secrecy they had given. Æschylus was indicted for having disclosed in the theatre certain details of the Mysteries, and he only escaped punishment by proving that he had never been initiated and, therefore, could not have violated any obligation. A Greek scholiast says that in five of his tragedies Æschylus spoke of Demeter and therefore may be supposed in these cases to have touched upon subjects connected with the Mysteries, and Heraclides of Pontus says that on this account he was in danger of being killed by the populace if he had not fled for refuge to the altar of Dionysos and been begged off by the Areopagites and acquitted on the ground of his exploits at Marathon. An accusation was brought against Aristotle of having performed a funeral sacrifice in honour of his wife in imitation of the Eleusinian ceremonies. Alcibiades was charged with mimicking the sacred Mysteries in one of his drunken revels, when he represented the hierophant; Theodorus, one of his friends, represented the herald; and another, Polytion, represented the dadouchos; other companions attending as initiates and being addressed as mystæ. The information against him ran:—

"Thessalus, the son of Cimon, of the ward of Lacais, accuseth Alcibiades, the son of Clinian, of the ward of Scambonis, of sacrilegiously offending the goddess Ceres and her daughter, Persephone, by counterfeiting their Mysteries and showing them to his companions in his own house, wearing such a robe as the high priest does when he shows the holy things; he called himself high priest; as did Polytion torch-bearer; and Theodorus, of the ward of Thyges, herald; and the rest of his companions he called persons initiated and Brethren of the Secret; therein acting contrary to the rules and ceremonies established by the Eumolpides, the Heralds and Priests at Eleusis."

Alcibiades did not appear in answer to the charge, and he was condemned in his absence, an order being made that his goods were to be confiscated. This occurred in 415 B.C. and the incident created quite a panic, as many prominent citizens, Andocides included, were implicated. "This man," said the accuser of Andocides, "vested in the same costume as a hierophant, has shown the sacred objects to men who were not initiated and has uttered words which it is not permissible to repeat." Andocides admitted the charge, but turned king's evidence, and named certain others as culprits with him. He was rewarded with a free pardon under a decree which Isotmides had issued, but those whom he named were either put to death or outlawed and their goods were confiscated. Andocides afterwards entered the temple while the Mysteries were in progress and was charged with breaking the law in so doing. He defended himself before a court of heliasts, all of whom had been initiated into the Mysteries, the president of the court being the Archon Basileus. The indictment was lodged by Cephisius, the chief prosecutor, with the Archon Basileus, during the celebration of the Greater Mysteries and while Andocides was still at Eleusis. Andocides was acquitted, and it is stated that Cephisius having failed to obtain one-fifth of the votes of the court, the result, according to the law, was that he had to pay a fine of a thousand drachmas and to suffer permanent exclusion from the Eleusinian shrine. Diagiras was accused of railing at the sanctity of the Mysteries of Eleusis in such a manner as to deter persons from seeking initiation, and a reward of one talent was offered to any one who should kill him or two talents to any one who should bring him alive. The Greek talent was of the value of about £200.

An ancient theme of oratorical composition and one set even in the sixth century of the Christian era ran :—

"The law punishes with death whoever has disclosed the Mysteries : some one to whom the initiation has been revealed in a dream asks one of the initiated if what he has seen is in conformity with reality: the initiate acquiesces by a movement of the head ; and for that he is accused of impiety."

Every care, therefore, was taken to prevent the secrecy of the Mysteries from being broken and the ceremonial becoming known to any not initiated. Details have, nevertheless, come to light in various ways, but chiefly through the ancient writings and inscriptions. Step by step and piece by piece the diligent researcher has been rewarded by the discovery of disconnected and isolated fragments which, by themselves, supply no precise information, but, taken in the aggregate, form a perfect mosaic. Though it was strictly forbidden to reveal what took place within the sacred enclosure and in the Hall of Initiation, it was permissible to state clearly the main object of initiation and the advantages to be derived from the act. Not only was the breaking of the obligation of secrecy given by an initiate visited with severe, sometimes even with capital, punishment, but the forcing of the temple enclosure by the uninitiated, as sometimes happened, was an offence of an equally impious and heinous character. By virtue of the unwritten laws and customs dating back to the most remote periods the penalty of death was frequently pronounced for faults not grave in themselves, although the forcing of the temple enclosure was, of course, a grave crime, but because they concerned religion. It was probably by virtue of those unwritten laws that the priests ordered the death of two young Arcananians who had penetrated, through ignorance, into the sacred precincts. They happened inadvertently to mix with the crowd at the season of the Mysteries and to enter the temple, but the questions asked by them, in consequence of their ignorance of the proceedings, betrayed them, and their intrusion was punished with death. This was in 200 B.C., and Rome made war upon Philip V of Macedonia on the complaint of the government of Athens against that king who wished to punish them for having rigorously applied the ancient laws to those two offenders, who were found guilty merely of entering the sanctuary at Eleusis without having previously been initiated. No judicial penalty, however, was meted out to the fanatical Epicurean eunuch who, with the object of proving that the gods had no existence, forced himself blaspheming into that part of the sanctuary into which the hierophant and the hierophantide alone had the right of entry. Ælianus states that a divine punishment in the form of a disease alone overtook him. Horace declared that he would not risk his life by going on to the water with a companion who had revealed the secret of the Mysteries.

The two days prior to initiation into the second and third degrees were spent by the candidates in solitary retirement and in strict fasting. It was a "retreat" in the strictest sense of the word. Fasting was practised, not only in imitation of the sufferings of Demeter when searching for Persephone, but because of the danger of the contact of holy things with unholy, the clean with the unclean. This also is one of the reasons why it was held to be impious even to speak of the Mysteries to one who had not been initiated and especially dangerous to allow such unclean and profane persons to take any part, even that of a viewer, in the ceremonies. Hence the punishment meted out by the State was in lieu of, or to avert, the divine wrath which such pollution might bring on the community at large.

At the entrance to the temple tablets were placed containing a list of forbidden foods. The list included several kinds of fish—the whistle-fish, gurnet, crab, and mullet. In all probability the whistle-fish is that known as *Sciæna aquila*, a Mediterranean fish that makes a noise under the water which has been compared to bellowing, buzzing, purring, or whistling, the air bladder being the sound-producing organ. The fish was greatly esteemed by the Romans. There is a large *Sciæna*, not *aquila*, though very like it, in the Fish Gallery of the British Museum (Natural History) opposite the entrance from the Zoological Library. The whistle-fish and crab were held to be impure, the first because it laid its eggs through the mouth, and the second because it ate filth which other fish rejected. The gurnet was rejected because of its fecundity as witnessed in its annual triple laying of eggs, but, according to some writers, it was rejected because it ate a fish which was poisonous to mankind. It may well be that other fish were interdicted, but Porphyry was probably exaggerating when he said that all fish were forbidden. Birds bred at home, such as chickens and pigeons, were also on the banned list, as were beans and certain vegetables which were forbidden for a mystical reason which Pausanias said he dare not reveal save to the initiated. The probable reason was that they were connected in some way with the wanderings of Demeter. Pomegranates were, of course, forbidden, from the incident of the eating of the pomegranate seeds by Persephone.

The candidates were carefully instructed in these rules before the beginning of the celebration. Originally the instruction of the candidates was in the hands of the hierophant, who, following the example of his ancestor, Eumolpus, claimed the privilege of preparing the candidates as well as that of communicating to them the knowledge of the divine Mysteries. But the continually increasing number of candidates made it necessary to employ auxiliary instructors, and this particular work was handed over to the charge of the mystagogues, who prepared the candidates either singly or in groups, the hierophant reserving to himself the general direction of the instruction. In the course of the initiation ceremony certain words had to be spoken by the candidates, and these were made known to them in advance, although, of course, apart from their context.

Admission to the second degree took place during the night between the sixth and seventh days of the celebration of the Mysteries, the candidates being led blindfolded into the temple and the ceremony opened with prayers and sacrifices by the second Archon. The candidates were crowned with myrtle wreaths, and, on entering the building, they purified themselves in a formal manner by immersing their hands in the consecrated water. Salt, laurel-leaves, barley, and crowns of flowers were also employed in the purification. The priests, vested in their sacerdotal garments, then came forward to receive the candidates. This initial ceremony took place in the outer hall of the temple, the temple itself being closed. A herald then came forward and uttered the proclamation: "Begone ye profane. Away from here, all ye that are not purified, and whose souls have not been freed from sin." In later years this formulary was changed, and in its stead the herald proclaimed: "If any atheist, or Christian, or Epicurean, is come to spy on the orgies, let him instantly retire, but let those who believe remain and be initiated, with good future." It was the final opportunity for the retirement of any who were not votaries who had by chance entered the precincts: if discovered afterwards the punishment was death. In order to make certain that no intruders remained behind all who were present had to answer certain specified questions. Then all again immersed their hands into the consecrated water and renewed their pledge of secrecy. The candidates for initiation then took off their ordinary garments and put on the skins of young does. This done, the priests wished them joy of all the happiness their initiation would bring them, and then left the candidates alone. Within a few minutes the apartment in which they were was plunged in total darkness. Lamentations and strange noises were heard; terrific peals of thunder resounded, seemingly shaking the very foundations of the temple; vivid flashes of lightning lit up the darkness, rendering it more terrible, while a more persistent light from a fire displayed fearful forms. Sighs, groans, and cries of pain resounded on all sides, like the shrieks of the condemned in Tartarus. The novitiates were taken hold of by invisible hands, their hair was torn, and they were beaten and thrown to the ground. Then a faint light became visible in the distance and a fearful scene appeared before their eyes. The gates of Tartarus were opened and the abode of the condemned lay before them. They could hear the cries of anguish and the vain regrets of those to whom Paradise was lost for ever. They could, moreover, witness their hopeless remorse: they saw, as well as heard, all the tortures of the condemned. The Furies, armed with relentless scourges and flaming torches, drove the unhappy victims incessantly to and fro, never letting them rest for a moment. Meanwhile the loud voice of the hierophant, who represented the judge of the earth, could be heard expounding the meaning of what was passing before them, and warning and threatening the initiates. It may well be imagined that all these fearful scenes were so terrifying that very frequently beads of anguish appeared on the brows of the novices. Howling dogs and even material demons are said actually to have appeared to the initiates before the scene was changed. Proclus, in his *Commentary on Alcibiades*, says: " In the most holy of the Mysteries, before the presence of the god, certain terrestrial demons are hurled forth, which call the attention from undefiled advantages to matter." At length the gates of Tartarus were closed, the scene was suddenly changed, and the innermost sanctuary of the temple lay open before the initiates in dazzling light. In the midst stood the statue of the goddess Demeter brilliantly decked and gleaming with precious stones; heavenly music entranced their souls; a cloudless sky overshadowed them; fragrant perfumes arose; and in the distance the privileged spectators beheld flowering meads, where the blessed danced and amused themselves with innocent games and pastimes. Among other writers the scene has been described by Aristophanes in *The Frogs* :—

Heracles. The voyage is a long one. For you will come directly to a very big lake of abysmal depth.

Dionysos. Then how shall I get taken across it?

Heracles. In a little boat just so high: an old man who plies that boat will take you across for a fee of two oboles.

Dionysos. Oh dear! How very powerful those two oboles are all over the world. How did they manage to get here?

Heracles. Theseus brought them. After this you will see serpents and wild beasts in countless numbers and very terrible. Then a great slough and overflowing dung; and in this you'll see lying any one who ever yet at any place wronged his guest or beat his mother, or smote his father's jaw, or swore an oath and foreswore himself. . . . And next a breathing of flutes shall be wafted around you, and you shall see a very beautiful light, even as in this world, and myrtle groves, and happy choirs of men and women, and a loud clapping of hands.

Dionysos. And who are these people, pray?
Heracles. The initiated.

It was regarded as permissible to describe certain scenes of the initiation, and this has been done by many writers, but a complete silence was demanded as to the means employed to realize the end, the rites and ceremonies in which the initiate took part, the emblems which were displayed, and the actual words uttered, and the slightest contravention of this rule rendered the offender liable to the strongest possible condemnation and chastisement.

In the course of the ceremony the hierophant asked the candidates a series of questions, to which written answers had been prepared and committed to memory by the candidates. The holy Mysteries were revealed to them from a book called *Petroma,* a word derived from *petra,* a stone, and so called because the writings were kept between two cemented stones which fitted in to each other. The Pheneatians used to swear by and on the Petroma. The domed top held within it a mask of Demeter which the hierophant wore at the celebration of the Mysteries, or during part of the ceremonial. The garments worn by the initiates during the ceremony were accounted sacred and equal to incantations and charms in their power to avert evils. Consequently they were never cast off until torn and tattered. Nor was it usual, even then, to throw them away, but it was customary to make them into swaddling clothes for children or to consecrate them to Demeter and Persephone.

Admission to the third degree took place during the night between the seventh and eighth days of the celebration of the Greater Mysteries. This, the final degree, with the exception of those called to be hierophants, was known as the degree of Epopta. Exactly in what the ceremonial consisted, save in one particular presently to be described, is unknown. Hippolytus is practically the only authority for the main incident of the degree. Certain words and signs were, however, communicated to the initiated which, it was stated, would, when pronounced at the hour of death, ensure the eternal happiness of the soul.

The most solemn part of the ceremony was that which has been described by some writers as the hierogamy, or sacred marriage of Zeus and Demeter, although some have erroneously referred to it as the marriage of Pluto and Persephone. During the celebration of the Mysteries the hierophant and hierophantide descended into a cave or deep recess and, after remaining there for a time, they returned to the assembly, surrounded seemingly by flames, and the hierophant, displaying to the gaze of the initiated an ear of corn, exclaimed with a loud voice: "The divine Brimo has given birth to the holy child Brimos: The strong has brought forth strength." The scene was dramatic and symbolical, and there could have been nothing material in the incident. The torches of the multitude were extinguished while the throng above awaited with anxious suspense the return of the priest and priestess from the murky place into which they had descended, for they believed their own salvation to depend upon the result of the mystic congress. The charges brought against the Eleusinian Mysteries of rioting and debauchery during their Grecian history are brought by those who were not permitted to share their honours, or who were prejudiced in favour of some other form of religion. In the opinion of the majority of contemporary writers these charges were wholly gratuitous, and they maintain that the Eleusinian Mysteries produced a sanctity of manners and a cultivation of virtue. They could not, of course, make a man virtuous against his will and Diogenes, when asked to submit to initiation, replied that Pataecion, a notorious robber, had obtained initiation.

"The Athenians," says Hippolytus, "in the initiation of Eleusis, show to the epoptæ the great, admirable, and most perfect mystery of the epoptæ: an ear of corn gathered in silence." The statement is so clear as to leave no doubt whatever on the subject; indeed, it has never been called into question.

The presentation of the ear of corn was regarded as a special, indeed the most important, feature of the Mysteries of Eleusis, and it was reserved for the final degree. Much has been made of this incident by many who can see no beauty in pre-Christian or non-Christian systems of religion, their comments being based mainly on a statement of Gregory Nazianus, who stands almost alone in discerning lewdness in the Eleusinian ceremonial. He says: "It is not in our religion that you will find a seduced Cora, a wandering Demeter, a Keleos, and a Triptolemus appearing with serpents; that Demeter is capable of certain acts and that she permits others. I am really ashamed to throw light on the nocturnal orgies of the initiations. Eleusis knows as well as the witnesses the secret of the spectacle, which is with reason kept so profound."

Apart from this isolated statement the Eleusinian Mysteries have not been charged, as many other ancient rites were, with promoting and encouraging immorality. In his account of the doings of the false prophet Alexander of Abountichos, Lucian describes how the impostor instituted rites which were a close parody of those celebrated at Eleusis, and he narrates the details of the travesty. Among the mimetic performances were not only the epiphany and birth of a god but the enactment of a sacred marriage. All preliminaries were gone through, and Lucian says that but for the abundance of lighted torches the marriage would actually have been consummated. The part of the hierophant was taken by the false prophet himself. From the travesty it is evident that in the genuine Mysteries, in silence, in darkness, and in perfect chastity the sacred marriage was symbolized and that immediately afterwards the hierophant came forward and standing in a blaze of torchlight made the announcement to the initiates.

The name *Brimo*, expressed at full length *Obrimo*, seems to be a variation of the compound term *Ob-Rimon*, "the lofty serpent goddess."

> The birth of Brimo; and the mighty deeds
> Of the Titanic hosts; the servitude
> Of Jove; and the mysterious mountain rites
> Of Cybelè, when with distracted pace she sought
> Through the wide world the beauteous Proserpine;
> The far-fam'd labours of the Machian Hercules;
> Th' Idèan orgies; and the giant force
> Of the dread Corybantes; and the wanderings
> Of Ceres, and the woes of Prosperpine:
> With these I sung the gifts of the Cabiri;
> The Mysteries of Bacchus; and the praise
> Of Lemnos, Samothrace, and lofty Cyprus,
> Fair Adonean Venus; and the rites
> Of dread Ogygian Praxidicè;
> Arinian Minerva's nightly festival;
> And Egypt's sorrow for the lost Osiris.
>
> *Orphic Hymn.*

Dr. Jevons maintains that this ear of corn was the totem of Eleusis, and this view has been adopted by M. Reinach, who says: "We find in the texts a certain trace not only of the cult but of the adoration and the exaltation (in the Christian meaning of the word) of the ear of corn." But he has omitted to quote the texts on which he relies for this assertion. It would be interesting to know why, among all the plants which die and revive in the course of a year, wheat was chosen for preference, why the ear more than the grain, why it should be emphasized that it was gathered, for what reason the spectacle was reserved for the epoptæ, and in what manner it secured or ensured for the individual a blissful existence after death. The demonstration presupposes that the preceding rites were leading up to this supreme display.

After this demonstration the epoptæ partook of barley meal flavoured with pennyroyal, as a solemn form of communion with Demeter. According to Eustathius, the compound was a kind of thick gruel, half-solid, half-liquid. This done, each of the initiated repeated after the hierophant the following words: "I have fasted, I have drank 'cyceon.' I have taken from the cystos, and after having tasted of it I placed it in the calathos. I again took it from the calathos and put it back in the cystos." This formula, notwithstanding its length, is said to have been the password leading to the third degree.

Justin Martyr gives the oath of initiation as

follows: "So help me heaven, the work of God who is great and wise: so help me the word of the Father which he spake when he established the whole universe in his wisdom."

With this ceremony the third degree ended, save that the epoptæ were placed upon exalted seats, around which the priests circled in mystic dances, The day succeeding admission into the final degree was regarded as a rigorous fast, at the conclusion of which the epoptæ drank of the mystic cyceon and ate of the sacred cakes.

According to Theo of Smyrna, the full or complete initiation consisted of five steps or degrees, which he sets out as follows:—

"Again, philosophy may be called the initiation into true sacred ceremonies, and the tradition of genuine mysteries; for there are five parts of initiation; the first of which is previous purgation, for neither are the Mysteries communicated to all who are willing to receive them, but there are certain characters who are prevented by the voice of the crier, such as those who possess impure hands and an inarticulate voice, since it is necessary that such as are not expelled from the Mysteries should first be refined by certain purgations, but after purgation the tradition of the sacred rite succeeds. The third part is denominated inspection. And the fourth, which is the end and design of inspection, is the binding of the head and fixing the crown, so that the initiated may, by this means, be enabled to communicate to others the sacred rites in which he has been instructed. Whether after this he becomes a torch-bearer, or an interpreter of the Mysteries, or sustains some other part of the sacerdotal office. But the fifth, which is produced from all these, is friendship with divinity, and the enjoyment of that felicity which arises from intimate converse with the gods. According to Plato, purification is to be derived from the five mathematical disciplines, viz. arithmetic, geometry, stereometry, music, and astronomy."

Apuleius is represented as saying to himself :—

"I approached the confines of death ; and, having crossed the threshold of Proserpine, I at length returned, borne along through all the elements. I beheld the sun shining in the dead of night with luminous splendour : I saw both the infernal and the celestial gods. I approached and adored them."

Themistius represents initiation in the following words :—

"Entering now the mystic dome, he is filled with horror and amazement. He is seized with solicitude and a total perplexity. He is unable to move a step forward ; and he is at a loss to find the entrance to that road which is to lead him to the place he aspires to. But now, in the midst of his perplexity, the prophet (hierophant) suddenly lays open to him the space before the portals of the temple. Having thoroughly purified him, the hierophant now discloses to the initiated a region all over illuminated and shining with a divine splendour. The cloud and thick darkness are dispersed; and the mind, which before was full of disconsolate obscurity, now emerges, as it were, into day, replete with light and cheerfulness, out of the profound depth into which it had been plunged."

The fee for initiation was a minimum sum of fifteen drachmas (a drachma being of the value of 7¾d.), in addition to which there were the usual honoraria to be bestowed upon the various officials, to which reference has already been made. Presumably, also, gifts in kind were made to the principal officials, for an inscription of the fifth century B.C., found at Eleusis, reads:—

"Let the Hierophant and the Torch-bearer command that at the Mysteries the Hellenes shall offer first-fruits of their crops in accordance with ancestral usage. . . . To those who do these things there shall be many good things, both good and abundant crops, whoever of them do not injure the Athenians, nor the city of Athens, nor the two goddesses."

The Telestrion or Hall of Initiation, sometimes called "The Mystic Temple," was surrounded on all sides by steps, which presumably served as seats for the initiated while the sacred dramas and processions took place on the floor of the hall. These steps were partly built in and partly cut in the solid rock; in later times they appear to have been covered with marble. There were two doors on each side of the hall with the exception of the north-west, where the entrance was cut out of the solid rock, a rock terrace at a higher level adjoining it. This was probably the station of those not yet admitted to full initiation. The roof of the hall was carried by rows of columns which were more than once renewed. The Hall itself did not accommodate more than four thousand people. The building was perhaps more accurately described by Aristophanes, who called it: "The House that welcomed the Mystæ," and he carefully distinguished it from the Temple of Demeter. It was not the dwelling-place of any god, and it, therefore, did not contain any holy image. It was built for the celebration of a definite ritual, and the Eleusinian Hall of Initiation was therefore the only known *church* of antiquity, if by that term we mean the meeting-place of the congregation.

Mr. James Christie, in his work on *Greek Vases,* contends that the phantasmal scenes in the Mysteries were shown by transparencies, such as are yet used by the Chinese, Javanese, and Hindus.

V

THEIR MYSTICAL SIGNIFICANCE

LIFE, as we know it, was looked upon by the ancient philosophers as death. Plato considered the body as the sepulchre of the soul, and in the *Cratylus* acquiesces in the doctrine of Orpheus that the soul is punished through its union with the body. Empedocles, lamenting his connection with this corporeal world, pathetically exclaimed :—

For this I weep, for this indulge my woe,
That e'er my soul such novel realms should know.

He also calls this material abode, or the realms of generation,

a joyless region,
Where slaughter, rage, and countless ills reside.

Philolaus, the celebrated Pythagorean, wrote : " The ancient theologists and priests testify that the soul is united with the body for the sake of suffering punishment, and that it is buried in the body as in a sepulchre " ; while Pythagoras himself said : " Whatever we see when awake is death, and when asleep a dream."

This is the truth intended to be expressed in the Mysteries. Sallustius, the neo-Platonic philosopher, in his treatise *Peri Theon kai Kosmou,* "Concerning the gods and the existing state of things," explains the rape of Persephone as signifying the descent of the soul. Other writers have explained the real element of the Mysteries as consisting in the relations of the universe to the soul, more especially after death, or as intimating obscurely by splendid visions the felicity of the soul here and hereafter when purified from the defilements of a material nature. The intention of all mystic ceremonies, according to Sallustius, was to conjoin the world and the gods. Plotinus says that to be plunged into matter is to descend and then fall asleep. The initiate had to withstand the dæmons and spectres, which, in later times, illustrated the difficulties besetting the soul in its approach to the gods, so also the Uasarian had to repel or satisfy the mystic crocodiles, vipers, avenging assessors, dæmons of the gate, and other dread beings whom he encountered in his trying passage through the valley of the shadow of death. Pindar, speaking of the Eleusinian Mysteries, says: "Blessed is he who, on seeing those common concerns under the earth, knows both the end of life and the given end of Jupiter."

Psyche is said to have fallen asleep in Hades through rashly attempting to behold corporeal beauty, and the truth intended to be taught in the Eleusinian

Mysteries was that prudent men who earnestly employed themselves in divine concerns were, above all others, in a vigilant state, and that imprudent men who pursued objects of an inferior nature were asleep, and engaged only in the delusion of dreams; and that if they happened to die in this sleep before they were aroused they would be afflicted with similar, but still sharper, visions in a future state.

Matter was regarded by the Egyptians as a certain mire or mud. They called matter the dregs or sediment of the first life. Before the first purification the candidate for initiation into the Eleusinian Mysteries was besmeared with clay or mud which it was the object of the purification to wash away. It also intimated that while the soul is in a state of servitude to the body it lives confined, as it were, in bonds through the dominion of this Titanic life. Thus the Greeks laid great stress upon the advantages to be derived from initiation. Not only were the initiates placed under the protection of the State, but the very act of initiation was said to assist in the spreading of goodwill among men, keep the soul from sin and crime, place the initiates under the special protection of the gods, and provide them with the means of attaining perfect virtue, the power of living a spotless life, and assure them of a peaceful death and of everlasting bliss hereafter. The hierophants assured all who participated in the

Mysteries that they would have a high place in Elysium, a clearer understanding, and a more intimate intercourse with the gods, whereas the uninitiated would for ever remain in outer darkness. Indeed, in the third degree the epoptæ were said to be admitted to the presence of and converse with the goddesses Demeter and Persephone, under whose immediate care and protection they were said to be placed. Initiation was referred to frequently as a guarantee of salvation conferred by outward and visible signs and by sacred formulæ.

The Lesser Mysteries were intended to symbolize the condition of the soul while subservient to the body, and the liberation from this servitude, through purgative virtues, was what the wisdom of the Ancients intended to signify by the descent into Hades and the speedy return from those dark abodes. They were held to contain perfective rites and appearances and the tradition of the sacred doctrines necessary to the perfection or accomplishment of the most splendid visions. The perfective part, said Proclus, precedes initiation, as initiation precedes inspection.

"Hercules," said Proclus also in *Plat. Polit.*, "being purified by sacred initiations and enjoying undefiled fruits, obtained at length a perfect establishment among the gods"; that is, freed from the bondage of matter ascending beyond the reach of its hands.

Plutarch wrote :—

"To die is to be initiated into the great mysteries,

. . . Our whole life is but a succession of errors, of painful wanderings, and of long-journeys by tortuous ways, without outlet. At the moment of quitting it, fears, terrors, quiverings, mortal sweats, and a lethargic stupor come and overwhelm us; but, as soon as we are out of it, we pass into delightful meadows, where the purest air is breathed, where sacred concerts and discourses are heard; where, in short, one is impressed with celestial visions. It is there that man, having become perfect through his new initiation, restored to liberty, really master of himself, celebrates, crowned with myrtle, the most august mysteries, holds converse with just and pure souls, and sees with contempt the impure multitude of the profane or uninitiated, ever plunged and sinking itself into the mire and in profound darkness."

Dogmatic instruction was not included in the Mysteries; the doctrine of the immortality of the soul traces its origin to sources anterior to the rise of the Mysteries. At Eleusis the way was shown how to secure for the soul after death the best possible fate. The miracle of regeneration, rather than the eternity of being, was taught.

Plato introduces Socrates as saying: "In my opinion those who established the Mysteries, whoever they were, were well skilled in human nature. For in these rites it was of old signified to the aspirants that those who died without being initiated stuck fast in mire and filth; but that he who was purified and initiated should, at his death, have his habitation with the gods."

Plato, again, in the seventh book of the *Republic* says: "He who is not able by the exercise of his reason to define the idea of the good, separating it from all other objects and piercing as in a battle through every kind of argument; endeavouring to confute, not according to opinion but according to evidence, and proceeding with all these dialectical exercises with an unshaken reason—he who cannot accomplish this, would you not say that he neither knows the good itself, nor anything which is properly demonstrated good? And would you not assert that such a one when he apprehended it rather through the medium of opinion than of science, that in the present life he is sunk in sleep and conversant with delusions and dreams; and that before he is roused to a vigilant state he will descend to Hades, and be overwhelmed with sleep perfectly profound?"

Olympiodorus, in his MS. Commentary on the Georgias of Plato, says of the Elysian fields: "It is necessary to know that the fortunate islands are said to be raised above the sea. . . . Hercules is reported to have accomplished his last labour in the Hesperian regions, signifying by this that, having vanquished an obscure and terrestrial life, he afterwards lived in open day—that is, in truth and resplendent light. So that he who in the present state vanquishes as much as possible a corporeal life, through the exercise of the cathartic virtues, passes in reality into the fortunate islands of the soul, and lives surrounded with the bright splendours of truth and wisdom proceeding from the sun of good."

The esoteric teaching was not, of course, grasped by all the initiates; the majority merely recognized or grasped the exoteric doctrine of a future state of rewards and punishments. Virgil, in his description, in the *Æneid,* of the Mysteries, confines himself to the exoteric teaching. Æneas, having passed over the Stygian lake, meets with the three-headed Cerberus. By Cerberus must be understood the discriminative part of the soul, of which a dog, by reason of its sagacity, is an emblem. The three heads signify the intellective, dianœtic, and doxatic powers. "He dragg'd the three-mouth'd dog to upper day" —i.e. by temperance, continence, and other virtues he drew upwards the various powers of the soul. The teaching of the Mysteries was not in opposition to the ordinary creed: it deepened it rather, revived it in a spiritual manner and gave to religion a force and a power it had not hitherto possessed.

The fable of Persephone, as belonging to the Mysteries, was properly of a mixed nature, composed of all four species of fable—theological, physical, animistic, and material. According to the arcana of ancient theology, the Coric order—i.e. that belonging to Persephone—is twofold, one part supermundane and the other mundane.

Proclus says: "According to the rumour of theologists, who delivered to us the most holy Eleusinian Mysteries, Persephone abides on high, in those dwellings of her mother which she prepared for her in inaccessible places, exempt from the sensible world. But she likewise dwells with Pluto, administering terrestrial concerns, governing the recesses of the earth and imparting soul to beings which are of themselves inanimate and dead."

The Orphic poet describes Persephone as "the life and the death of mortals," and as being the mother of Eubuleus or Bacchus by an ineffable intercourse with Jupiter. Porphyry asserts that the wood pigeon was sacred to her and that she was the same as Maia, or the great mother, who is usually claimed as the parent of the Arkite god Mercury.

According to Nösselt the following may be taken as the meaning of the myth of Demeter and her lost daughter: "Persephone, the daughter of the all-productive earth (Demeter), is the seed. The earth rejoices at the sight of the plants and flowers, but they fade and wither, and the seed disappears quickly from the face of the earth when it is strewn on the ground. The dreaded monarch of the underworld has taken possession of it. In vain the mother searches for her child, the whole face of nature mourns her loss, and everything sorrows and grieves with her. But, secretly and unseen, the seed develops itself in the lap of the earth, and at length it starts forth: what was dead is now alive; the earth, all decked with fresh green, rejoices at the recovery of her long-lost daughter, and everything shares in the joy."

Demeter was worshipped in a twofold sense by the Greeks, as the foundress of agriculture and as goddess of law and order. They used to celebrate yearly in her honour the Thesmorphoria, or Festival of Laws. According to some ancient writers the Greeks, prior to the time of Demeter and Triptolemus, fed upon the acorns of the ilex, or the evergreen oak. Acorns, according to Virgil, were the food in Epiros, and in Spain, according to Strabo. The Scythians made bread with acorns. According to another tradition, before Demeter's time, men neither cultivated corn nor tilled the ground, but roamed the mountains and woods in search for the wild fruits which the earth produced. Isocrates wrote: "Ceres hath made the Athenians two presents of the greatest consequence: corn, which brought us out of a state of brutality; and the Mysteries, which teach the initiated to entertain the most agreeable expectations touching death and eternity." The coins of Eleusis represented Demeter in a car drawn by dragons or serpents which were sometimes winged. The goddess had two ears of corn in her right hand or, as some imagined, torches, indicating that she was searching for her daughter. George Wheler, in his *Journey into Greece*, published in

1682, says: "We observed many large stones covered with wheat-ears and bundles of poppy bound together; these being the characters of Ceres." At Copenhagen there is a statue representing Demeter holding poppies and ears of corn in her left hand. On a coin of Lampsacus of the fourth century B.C., Persephone is described in the act of rising from the earth.

According to Taylor, the Platonist, Demeter in the legend represents the evolution of that self-inspective part of our nature which we properly determine intellect, and Persephone that vital, self-moving, and animate part which we call soul. Pluto signifies the whole of our material nature, and, according to Pythagoras, the empire of this god commences downwards from the Galaxy or Milky Way.

Sallust says that among the mundane divinities Ceres is the deity of the planet Saturn. The cavern signifies the entrance into mundane life accomplished by the union of the soul with the terrestrial body. Demeter, who was afraid lest some violence be offered to Persephone on account of her inimitable beauty, conveyed her privately to Sicily and concealed her in a house built on purpose by the Cyclops, while she herself directed her course to the temple of Cybele, the mother of the gods. Here we see the first cause of the soul's descent, viz. her desertion of a life wholly according to intellect, occultly signified by the separation of Demeter and Persephone.

Afterwards Jupiter instructed Venus to go and betray Persephone from her retirement, that Pluto might be enabled to carry her away, and, to prevent any suspicion in the virgin's mind, he commanded Diana and Pallas to bear her company. The three goddesses on arrival found Persephone at work on a scarf for her mother, on which she had embroidered the primitive chaos and the formation of the world. Venus, says Taylor, is significant of desire, which, even in the celestial regions (for such is the residence of Persephone until she is ravished by Pluto), begins silently and fraudulently in the recesses of the soul. Minerva is symbolical of the rational power of the soul; and Diana represents nature, or the merely natural and vegetable part of our composition, both ensnared through the allurements of desire.

In Ovid we have Narcissus, the metamorphosis of a youth who fell a victim to love of his own corporeal form. The rape of Persephone, according to the Homeric Hymn to Demeter, was the immediate consequence of her gathering this wonderful flower. By Narcissus falling in love with his shadow in the limpid stream we behold the representation of a beautiful soul, which, by prolonged gaze upon the material form, becomes enamoured of a corporeal life and changed into a being consisting wholly of the mere energies of nature. Plato, forcing his passage through the earth, seizes on Persephone and carries her away, despite the resistance of Minerva and Diana, who were forbidden by Jupiter to attempt her deliverance after her abduction. This signifies that the lapse of the soul into a material nature is contrary to the genuine wish and proper condition. Pluto having hurried Persephone into the infernal regions, marriage succeeds. That is to say, the soul having sunk into the profoundities of a material nature, unites with the dark tenement of the material body. Night is with great beauty and propriety introduced, standing by the nuptial couch and confirming the oblivious league. That is to say, the soul, by union with a material body, becomes familiar with darkness and subject to the empire of night, in consequence of which she dwells wholly with delusive phantoms and till she breaks her fetters is deprived of the perception of that which is real and true.

The nine days of the Festival are said to be significant of the descent of the soul. The soul, in falling from her original, divine abode in the heavens, passes through eight spheres, viz. the inerratic sphere and the seven planets, assuming a different body and employing different energies in each, finally becoming connected with the sublunary world and a terrene body on the ninth. Demeter and the foundation of the art of tillage are said to signify the descent of intellect into the realms of generation, the greatest benefit and ornament which a material nature is capable of receiving. Without the possibility of the participation of intellect in the lower material sphere nothing but an irrational and a brutal life would subsist.

But, according to some writers, the initiates into the third degree were taught that the gods and goddesses were only dead mortals, subject while alive to the same passions and infirmities as themselves; and they were taught to look upon the Supreme Cause, the Creator of the Universe, as pervading all things by His virtue and governing all things by His power. Thus the meaning of *Mystes* is given as "one who sees things in disguise," and that of *Epopt* as "one who sees things as they are, without disguise." The Epopt, after passing through the ceremonial of exaltation, was said to have received Autopsia, or complete vision. Virgil declared that the secret of the Mysteries was the Unity of the Godhead, and Plato owned it to be "difficult to find the Creator of the Universe, and, when found, impossible to discover Him to all the world." Varro, in his work *Of Religions*, says that "there were many truths which it was inconvenient for the State to be generally known; and many things which, though false, it was expedient the people should believe, and that, therefore, the Greeks shut up their Mysteries in the silence of their sacred enclosures." The Mysteries declared that the future life was not the shadowy, weary existence which it had hitherto been supposed to be, but that through the rites of purification and sacrifices of a sacramental character man could secure a better hope for the future. Thus the Eleusinian Mysteries became the chief agent in the conversion of the Greek world from the Homeric view of Hades to a more hopeful belief as to man's state after death. Tully promulgated a law forbidding nocturnal sacrifices in which women were permitted to take part, but made an express exception in favour of the Eleusinian Mysteries, giving as his reason: "Athens hath produced many excellent, even divine inventions and applied them to the use of life, but she has given nothing better than those Mysteries by which we are drawn from an irrational and savage life and tamed, as it were, and broken to humanity. They are truly called *Initia*, for they are indeed the beginnings of a life of reason and virtue."

Secrecy was enjoined because it was regarded as essential that the profane should not be permitted to share the knowledge of the true nature of Demeter and Persephone, as if it were known that these goddesses were only mortal women their worship would become contemptible. Cicero says that it was the humanity of Demeter and Persephone, their places of interment, and several facts of a like nature that were concealed with so much care. Diagoras, the Melian, was accounted an atheist because he revealed the real secret of the Eleusinian

Mysteries. The charge of atheism was the lot of any who communicated a knowledge of the one, only God. Pindar says, referring to the Mysteries: "Happy is he who has seen these things before leaving this world: he realizes the beginning and the end of life, as ordained by Zeus"; and Sophocles wrote: "Oh, thrice blessed the mortals, who, having contemplated these Mysteries, have descended to Hades; for those only will there be a future life of happiness—the others there will find nothing but suffering."

BIBLIOGRAPHY

Andocides. *De Mysteriis.*
Antiquities of Ionia.
Apollodorus.
Aristides.
Aristophanes.
Aristotle. *Nico. Ethics.*
Arnobius. *Disputationes adversus Gentes.*

Barthelemy. *Voyage du Jeune Anacharsis en Grèce*
Blackwood's Magazine, 1853.

Chandler. *Travels in Greece.*
Cheetham, S. *Mysteries, Pagan and Christian.*
Cicero.
Clement of Alexandria.
Contemporary Review, 1880.
Cornutus. *Theologiæ Græcæ Compendium.*
Corpus inscript. Attic.
Corpus inscript. Gr.

d'Aliviella. *Eleusinia.*
Decharme. *Mythologie de la Grèce antique.*
Diodorus Siculus.
Dion Cassius.
Dodwell. *Tour.*
Duncan. *Religions of Profane Antiquity.*
Dyer. *The Gods in Greece.*

Encyclopædia Britannica.
Eunapius. *Vita Maxim.*
Eusebius. *Preparatio Evangelii.*

Farnell. *Cults of the Greek States.*
Firmicus Maternus. *De errore profanarum religionum.*
Foucart. *Les mystères d'Eleusis.*
Frazer. *Golden Bough.*

Gardner. *New Chapters in Greek History.*
Gardner and Jevons. *Manual of Greek Antiquities.*
Gibbon.
Gregory of Nazianzus.
Grote. *History of Greece.*
Guerber, H. A. *Myths of Greece and Rome.*

Harrison, J. E. *Prolegomena.*
Hatch, Edwin. *Hibbert Lectures.*
Herodianus.
Herodotus.
Hippolytus.
Horace.

International Folk Lore Congress, 1891. *Papers and Transactions.*
Isocrates.

Lactantius.
Lang, Andrew. *Myth, Ritual, and Religion.*
Ditto. *Translation of Homeric Hymns.*
Lenormant, F. *Eleusis.*
Libanius.
Livy.
Lobeck. *Aglaophamus.*
Lucian. *Dialogues of the Dead.*
Lysias. *Contra Andocidem.*

Mahaffy, J. P. *Rambles and Studies in Greece.*
Mannhardt, W. *Mythologische Forschungen.*
Meursius.
Maury, A. *Les Religions de la Grèce.*

Mommsen. *Feste der Stadt Athen in Altertum.*
Ditto. *Heortologie.*

Nösselt and Hall. *Mythology, Greek and Roman.*

Olympiodorus.

Pater, Walter. *Greek Studies.*
Paton, W. R. *The Holy Names of the Eleusinian Priests.*
Pausanius. *Description of Greece.*
Philios, Demetrius. *Eleusis, ses mystères, ses ruines, et son musée.*
Phlégon de Tralles. *Frag. hist. gr.*
Pindar.
Plato.
Plethos.
Plotinus.
Plutarch.
Pollux.
Philostratus. *Appollonius of Tyana.*
Porphyry.
Preller. *Demeter und Persephone.*
Preller-Robert. *Griechische Mythologie.*
Pringsheim. *Arch. Beitrage.*
Proclus.

Reinach. *Cultes, mythes, et Religions.*
Revue de l'histoire des Religions.
Revue de Philologie, 1893.
Revue des études grecques, 1906.
Rohde, E. *Psyche.*

Saglio-Pottier. *Dictionnaire des Antiquités.*
Sallustius.
Schömann. *Griechische Antherthümer.*
Sophocles.

Strabo.
Suetonius.
Suidas.

Taylor, T. *The Eleusinian and Bacchic Rites.*
Ditto. *The Mystical Hymns of Orpheus.*
Tertullian.
Themistius.
Theodoretus.

Varro. *Of Religions.*
Virgil.
Voltaire.

Waechter. *Reinheitsvorschriften.*
Welcker, F. G. *Griechische Götterlehre.*
Wheler. *Journey into Greece.*

Xenophon.